Part One

Healing Hearts in the Shadows of Forbidden Love

Part Two

Overcoming Obstacles on the Road to Romance

By Willy Lapse Laguerre

HEALING HEARTS IN THE SHADOWS OF FORBIDDEN LOVE

First edition. November 13, 2024.

ISBN: 979-8230775720

Written by Willy Lapse Laguerre.

Also by Willy Lapse Laguerre

Cultural Differences
The Forbidden Love

Deception
A Hustler's Journey - Against The Shadow

Fairy Tales Story
The King of Milk Tome 1
The Child Of Shadows

Poetry
Where The Shadow Can not Reach

Relationship
The Game You Can Never Win

Romance

Healing Hearts In The Shadows Of Forbidden Love

The Shattered Veil

The Valley Of The Masks

Thriller Horror

Station 13

DEDICATION

For those who dare to love beyond limits,

who find beauty in the unknown,

and who choose connection over convention—

this story is for you.

CONTENTS

Chapter 1: Whispers of a New Beginning

Chapter 2: Feeling the Pull

Chapter 3: Moments of Clarity

Chapter 4: Hidden Cracks

Chapter 5: Forbidden Echoes

Chapter 6: In the Shadows of Doubt

Chapter 7: Finding Resilience

Chapter 8: Healing Together

Chapter 9: Embracing Change

Chapter 10: A Love Reimagined

Foreword

Love is a universal language, timeless and transcendent, yet it often dances on the precipice of convention. Some stories breathe life into the forbidden, ones where love does not fit neatly within the confines of societal norms. These stories ignite our imaginations, challenge our perceptions, and remind us of the complexity of human connection. *"Unveiling a Love That Defies Conventions"* is one such tale—a tender yet tumultuous journey into the heart of forbidden love.

At its core, this narrative delves into the life of Lily, a spirited sixteen-year-old navigating the delicate threshold between adolescence and adulthood. Like many her age, Lily lives within the structured rhythms of her small town—a place where life follows a predictable cadence, tethered by expectations and an innate resistance to change. But beneath her seemingly ordinary existence lies a yearning for something extraordinary. This unspoken desire propels her into the arms of the enigmatic stranger, Jack, and into a world of possibilities she never imagined.

The park, serene and unassuming, is the crucible for their connection. Among blooming flowers and the rustle of leaves, Lily first notices Jack. With his intense gaze fixed on the pages of a worn book, he exudes an otherworldly quality. He is unlike the boys Lily has grown accustomed to—his demeanor carries a quiet confidence that speaks of a life outside the narrow confines of their insular town. The intrigue Jack evokes in Lily sets the stage for a love that is both thrilling and fraught with uncertainty.

In many ways, Jack represents the unknown—a gateway to experiences that transcend Lily's sheltered upbringing. But his mystery is not without weight. Though concealed beneath a veneer of charm, his secrets cast long shadows over their burgeoning bond. Jack is a puzzle, and Lily is drawn to the challenge of piecing him together, even as she senses the potential peril of delving too deeply.

Their first conversation, seemingly innocuous, sparks a connection that is anything but trivial. In Jack, Lily finds an intellectual equal who shares her love for literature and opens her eyes to a world far beyond her own. Their dialogue flows effortlessly, bridging the gap between their disparate lives. Jack's tales of travel and personal upheaval ignite a spark in Lily's imagination, fueling her desire to step beyond the boundaries of her safe yet stifling world.

But as with all forbidden love stories, their path is riddled with obstacles. The whispers of town gossip, the judgmental gazes of peers, and the disapproving murmurs of Lily's friends form a chorus of dissent. Despite this, Lily cannot resist the pull of Jack's magnetism. Her days become consumed with thoughts of him, and the park transforms into a sacred space where their connection can flourish, away from the prying eyes of a society intent on enforcing its rules.

Jack's reluctance to reveal the full extent of his past adds a layer of tension to their relationship. His disappearances, though brief, weigh heavily on Lily's heart, leaving her torn between trust and doubt. Yet, in these moments of uncertainty, the depth of her feelings becomes clear. Love, she realizes, is not about perfection but about the willingness to embrace the imperfections of another.

This story explores the intoxicating highs of first love and its inherent complexities. Through Lily's eyes, we witness the beauty of vulnerability—the courage it takes to open one's heart, even in the face of potential pain. Her journey is a testament to the resilience of the human spirit and the transformative power of connection.

The societal pressures looming over their relationship heighten the emotional stakes. Jack and Lily's love exists in defiance of the status quo, challenging the rigid structures that dictate who they should be and whom they should love. Their decision to meet in secrecy is both a rebellion and a retreat, a means of preserving their fragile bond in a world that seeks to tear it apart.

Amid these challenges, Lily discovers the profound truths that come with loving someone deeply. She learns that love is not a sanctuary from the trials of life but a crucible that tests and refines the soul. Jack becomes both her refuge and her most significant uncertainty—a paradox that mirrors the duality of love itself.

The title, *"Unveiling a Love That Defies Conventions,"* is apt, for this story is as much about revelation as it is about romance. It is a journey of self-discovery for Lily, who must confront the external forces that threaten her happiness and her fears and insecurities. Through her relationship with Jack, she understands the fragility and strength of the human heart.

What makes this story particularly compelling is its universal resonance. While the specifics of Lily and Jack's experiences are unique, the emotions they evoke are deeply familiar. Who among us has not longed for a connection that transcends the ordinary? Who has not felt the bittersweet sting of loving against the odds? This tale reminds us that love, in all its forms, is a force to be reckoned with—a force that can illuminate even the darkest corners of our lives.

As readers, we are invited to witness the unfolding of Lily and Jack's relationship in all its raw, unfiltered beauty. Their love story is not a fairy tale but a mirror, reflecting the complexities of human emotion and the challenges of forging meaningful connections in an imperfect world. It is a story that will linger in your heart, urging you to reconsider what it means to love and be loved.

So, step into this world where love defies expectations and challenges the status quo. Allow yourself to be swept away by the intensity of Lily and Jack's bond, and let their journey inspire you to embrace the complexities of your own heart. This story will not only move you but also leave you pondering the true nature of love—its capacity to heal, challenge, and ultimately transform.

Welcome to *"Unveiling a Love That Defies Conventions."* May it remind you that even in a world of boundaries, love knows no limits.

ACKNOWLEDGMENTS

Writing a story as heartfelt and transformative as *"Unveiling a Love That Defies Conventions"* is never a solitary endeavor. It is the culmination of support, inspiration, and encouragement from so many who have touched my life in ways big and small. I am deeply grateful to everyone who contributed to this journey.

First and foremost, I extend my heartfelt thanks to my family, whose unwavering belief in me has been the cornerstone of my creative pursuits. Your love and encouragement have been the foundation upon which I've built not just this story but my entire writing career. To my parents, for fostering my imagination and encouraging me to chase my dreams, and to my siblings, for being my first readers and most honest critics—I owe so much of my success to you.

To my close friends, who have supported me through countless late-night brainstorming sessions and moments of self-doubt, your belief in me gave me the courage to see this story through. Thank you for listening to my ramblings about forbidden love, enigmatic strangers, and small-town life, and for never letting me give up, even when the writing process felt overwhelming.

I am especially grateful to my editor, whose keen eye and insightful feedback elevated this story to new heights. Your ability to challenge me while respecting my vision was a gift, and your guidance has been instrumental in shaping this book into something I am truly proud of.

To my publisher and the entire production team, thank you for your dedication and hard work. From cover design to marketing, your efforts have brought this story to life in ways I never could have imagined. Seeing my words translated into a tangible book has been a dream come true, and I am endlessly grateful for your expertise and passion.

I also wish to thank my readers, both new and returning. Your enthusiasm, feedback, and support are what keep me writing. This story was crafted with you in mind, and it is my deepest hope that it resonates with you and stays with you long after you've turned the final page.

Lastly, to anyone who has ever dared to love boldly, defy expectations, or chase something extraordinary despite the odds—this book is for you. It is your courage and vulnerability that inspired this story, and I am humbled to have had the privilege of putting it into words.

Thank you all from the bottom of my heart. This journey would not have been possible without you.

Chapter 1

Whispers of a New Beginning

I never believed in love at first sight until I met him that rainy afternoon. As the raindrops danced on the pavement, I couldn't shake the feeling that our encounter was monumental despite the shadows lurking around us.

In a world dictated by unyielding expectations, I was just a girl caught between the innocence of youth and the harsh realities of societal constraints, yearning for a love that felt dangerously exhilarating yet impossibly wrong. Every glance shared between us felt like an act of defiance; the whispers of disapproval echoed in my mind, reminding me of the walls built around our worlds, enclosing us in a reality where love was anything but free.

As our eyes met, the air was thick with unspoken words—a silent promise woven in the tension of hidden glances and fleeting touches that made my heart race. But beneath my heart's longing lay a storm brewing—a disruption of doubt, fear, and the gnawing realization that not every love story has a happy ending. Would our hearts withstand the tests that lay in wait?

Growing up, I often felt out of place within the confines of my own life. Though outwardly perfect, my home was a stage for underlying tensions that left me craving something more. It was a world where silence spoke louder than words, and loneliness lingered in rooms filled with people. My school was a maze of shifting alliances and whispered judgments. The hallways buzzed with gossip, each whisper acting as a reminder of how quickly one could fall from grace. Amidst this chaos,

I felt an overwhelming urge to find solace and forge connections that transcended superficial bonds.

Then, there was our culture, a tapestry woven with rules that dictated whom we could love. Our community held traditions dear, expecting unquestioning obedience and conformity. The weight of these invisible barriers pressed down on me, leaving little room to breathe, let alone venture into the forbidden territories of the heart. Yet, despite these constraints, or perhaps because of them, the desire to rebel against such norms began to simmer within me.

Enter the mysterious stranger. His presence shook the very foundations of my carefully constructed world. We collided beneath the gray skies, his enigmatic aura drawing me in like a moth to a flame. He seemed untouched by the shackles that bound me—an outsider whose secrets promised adventure and liberation beyond the mundane. Our meeting was serendipitous, lending a sense of magic to a dreary day. From that brief encounter, my nights were filled with dreams of what could be—fantasies spun from fleeting moments and stolen glances.

As I watched him leave, curiosity bubbled beneath the surface, gnawing at my insides. Who was he? Where did he come from, and why did he feel so familiar? These questions haunted my thoughts, echoing through the corridors of my mind. Our morning exchanges transformed into constant musings about his past and intentions, weaving stories around potential futures threaded with hope and uncertainty.

It wasn't long before those initial reactions gave way to deeper introspection. Mixed emotions rippled through me—attraction mingled with doubt, excitement danced alongside fear. This internal tug-of-war mirrored the complexity of first love; it felt like standing on the precipice of an unknown journey, unsure whether to lean into the thrill or retreat to the safety I had always known.

Despite the many shades of gray permeating my emotions, one thing remained clear: love, or whatever this was, demanded acknowledgment. With him, life sparkled with possibilities and risks, and each encounter was a chapter waiting to be written. The allure of stepping into his world proved irresistible. Beneath his aloofness lay glimpses of vulnerability that beckoned, urging me to uncover mysterious layers.

Yet, amidst this burgeoning connection, societal constraints loomed large. The whispers of disapproval from classmates and adults were stark reminders that venturing into uncharted territory was perilous. Each comment pierced through newfound optimism, tethering dreams to reality. Observing interactions among peers exposed the intricate dance between tradition and rebellion—a treacherous path that countless others had traversed before us.

Reflecting on these barriers forced me to confront my values—my willingness to challenge preconceived notions for something true yet ephemeral. The metaphorical walls surrounding us took shape, casting shadows over a budding romance not yet fully realized. Whether laden with symbolism or spoken aloud, each interaction represented mounting obstacles beneath the surface—themes of sacrifice, loyalty, and resilience interwoven through tales etched into time.

Would our clandestine affair defy expectations and flourish against all odds? Or would it crumble under the sheer weight of its unwieldy burden? These musings punctuated sleepless nights, filling the void with anticipation as much as apprehension.

Our love story, set against a backdrop saturated with societal norms, became a testament to the indomitable spirit of youth, unfurling its wings amid turbulent skies. Hearts destined to heal found solace in one another, discovering strength untapped before their union. Through laughter and tears, dreams and despair, we unearthed truths previously obscured by the noise of expectation.

And so, this tale of love and self-discovery begins. It's an invitation to join us on a journey where hearts dare to dream in the face of adversity, where healing emerges from the depths of shadowed spaces. Herein lies the chronicle of a young soul who braved storms to seek understanding, sparking inspiration among those grappling with tumultuous feelings and uncertainty.

For at its core, our narrative serves as a reminder that love, even when forged in darkness, holds the power to illuminate paths untraveled—an enduring promise to navigate life's complexities with courage and compassion.

Days passed, and the pull between us deepened. Each time I saw him, my heart raced a little faster, as if our connection were an unspoken spell we cast on each other. I found a spot to steal glances at him from across the cafeteria during lunch. His laughter rang out, drawing giggles from those surrounding him— a sweet sound I wanted to bottle up. I often wondered if he knew the effect he had on me or if he enjoyed the spotlight without seeing the weight of my gaze. The risks felt palpable, yet the thrill of not knowing what was next kept me lingering at the moment, hoping for one more smile, one more shared secret.

One afternoon, as the clouds rolled in, I decided to take a detour on my way home, hoping to run into him. I strolled, letting raindrops punctuate each step until I spotted him leaning against a brick wall, his eyes scanning the streets. He looked like a character straight out of a daydream. The rain intensified, soaking through my jacket, but I hardly noticed. The world around us faded, and in that moment, it felt like we were the only two people alive. Gathering courage, I approached him, feeling my cheeks warm. "Hey," I said, trying to sound casual despite the flutter in my chest. He turned toward me, and his face lit up as always when I appeared.

"I wondered if I'd run into you," he replied, his voice smooth and inviting. I felt a surge of gratitude for that simple statement. He leaned in closer, and it felt like the world's noise had paused for a brief moment—just the two of us, breathing in sync, hearts racing in tandem. "Want to escape the rain?" he suggested, his grin widening. I hesitated for a split second, imagining the repercussions of being seen with him—but the thought of refusing shattered beneath the weight of my eagerness. I nodded, and together, we dashed into a nearby café, laughter spilling out as we both stumbled inside.

In the cozy warmth, we found a quiet corner, and as we dripped water onto the floor, I felt my apprehensions begin to wash away. "So, what's your story?" I asked, leaning closer as I wrapped my hands around a mug of steaming chocolate. He raised an eyebrow, a playful challenge in his expression. "What makes you think I have a story worth telling?" he teased, but his smile betrayed him. I couldn't help but encourage him. "Everyone has a story," I insisted. "Especially someone like you."

His laughter echoed, and then he grew serious. "Alright, if you insist. I grew up here, but it feels like I've always been searching for where I belong. My parents... they have plans for me—plans that don't include this place." He paused, studying my reaction. I sensed the weight of his words, the yearning for freedom entwined with the chains of expectation. "You know what that feels like, right?"

"I do," I whispered, understanding the undertone of his confession all too well. "Sometimes it feels like living someone else's dream." He nodded, an unspoken alliance forming between us. My heart swelled as we shared more of ourselves—our fears, dreams, and the struggle for authenticity in a world that demanded compliance. Each revelation pulled me closer, weaving our lives together in an unexpected tapestry of empathy and hope.

As the rain drummed against the café windows, I knew this moment was pivotal. The connection between us was expanding, and I could sense something important shifting in our souls. "What if we just left?" he asked suddenly, a spark of mischief illuminating his eyes.

"What if we just took off and chased whatever lies ahead, no rules, no expectations?" I inhaled sharply, the idea igniting a flame inside me. The notion of escape, of chasing the wild unknown with him, sent shivers through my spine—thrilling and terrifying all at once.

"I could never," I countered playfully, though a part of me longed to say yes. "What about school? The future? Our families?" But even as I listed these reasons, I felt my resolve wavering. The draw to adventure pulled me in like a siren's song. "What if we don't have to decide right now?" he suggested, his expression softening. "What if we just... explore? Together?"

The warmth of his gaze ignited something raw within me. I felt seen and understood, and for the first time in a long while, I considered that maybe it was okay to risk it all for the chance of something real. "Okay," I said finally, my heart committing to the uncharted path. He smiled, and I couldn't help but smile back, the thrill of our shared secret hanging in the air like a promise.

With a rush of adrenaline, we plotted our first adventure. We would roam the town, hiding from expectations and immersing ourselves in moments stolen without fear. We slipped out of the café, the rain easing to a drizzle, and it felt like the beginning of something monumental. Each step we took felt charged like we were carving out new paths with every breath. In that swirling amalgamation of uncertainty and excitement, I dared to imagine who we might become as we chased the sunset together—free from constraints, basking in the beauty of the unknown.

Chapter 2
Feeling the Pull

Every young adult's heart lies within an intricate web of feelings as they take tentative steps into the world of love. Emotions swirl, sometimes soaring to dizzying heights while at other times crashing into confusion and uncertainty. This journey, filled with anticipation, excitement, and often heartbreak, is familiar to all who have ever experienced the intoxicating allure of a first crush or the bittersweet taste of love that defies the rules.

Our story begins in a world not unlike our own—where societal norms dictate who should and shouldn't be together. Here, we meet our protagonist, a young soul navigating the throes of adolescence, balancing on the precarious edge between childhood naiveté and adult understanding. When she encounters a mysterious stranger, an undeniable spark ignites, transcending the barriers laid before them by an often unyielding society.

Their bond deepens through moments that speak more vividly than words ever could. A glance across a crowded room, a shared smile that lingers too long, and the gentle brush of hands that leaves a trail of electricity—these instances weave a tapestry of silent communication that defies their surroundings. For those reading along, this will resonate deeply, echoing the heart-thumping excitement of a first infatuation that seems all-consuming.

As they navigate this newfound connection, shared experiences become the building blocks of their relationship. Conversations that reveal vulnerabilities and laughter that echoes with authenticity create a sanctuary for them both—a place where they can be themselves without fear of judgment. These interactions remind us that intimacy isn't built overnight but rather through moments of genuine connection that knit two souls together in a way mere proximity never could.

Yet, as palpable as their connection grows, so do the challenges that accompany it. Being near each other is both a blessing and a curse, stoking the flames of attraction while simultaneously complicating their lives. For many young readers, this friction will resonate, encapsulating the complexities of yearning for closeness yet fearing the consequences of being discovered in a world that might not be so forgiving.

A particular moment that makes one's heart race and time stand still becomes a turning point, solidifying their chemistry and underscoring the potent pull between them. This incident serves as a beacon within their developing narrative, revealing how love, forbidden or otherwise, can feel exhilarating and terrifying, often simultaneously. It's a moment destined to linger, foreshadowing the future choices they will need to face together.

However, beneath the surface, layers of emotions bubble within our protagonist—a swirling storm of contradictory feelings that paint a vivid picture of her internal landscape. The joy she feels in these stolen moments with her love clashes with the guilt imposed by society's rigid expectations. This duality reflects many young readers' struggles, often oscillating between happiness and remorse as they navigate their forbidden romances.

The constant undercurrent of anxiety about what others—peers, family, even the broader community—might think adds another dimension to her internal conflict. It's a pressure many will recognize, highlighting how fragile young love can be when subjected to outside scrutiny. This fear of judgment resonates with anyone seeking acceptance in a world that demands conformity over individuality.

Amidst this turmoil, the desire for acceptance tugs at her heartstrings, creating a fierce emotional conflict. She yearns to be true to herself and her feelings while also longing for the approval of those around her. This universal theme of belonging encourages readers to reflect on their struggles with identity and the desire to fit in while remaining authentic.

Adding to this mix is the age-old confusion between lust and love—a blur of passionate attraction that often complicates youthful emotions. This exploration offers layers to the character's development, mirroring the everyday experience of young adults trying to discern what love truly means amid the whirlwind of teenage life.

As our protagonist reflects on her desires and questions her choices, moments of introspection bring clarity amidst the chaos. Her journey is dotted with hesitation and self-doubt, relatable to anyone who has found themselves lost in thought, questioning their path. These reflections emphasize the importance of looking inward while navigating complex personal decisions.

Her physical reactions—heart racing, palms sweating—are involuntary betrayals of her internal conflict, making her struggle tangible and relatable. Readers will resonate with these visceral responses, recognizing the validity of their bodies' cues during emotional unrest.

External pressures from family and friends push against the desires of her heart, illustrating the clash between societal expectations and personal truths. This tension is all too familiar to those caught in the crossfire of wanting to follow their path while feeling tethered by the opinions of others.

Fear of the unknown looms large, casting shadows over potential futures. Yet, as the narrative unfolds, her growing resolve and determination to embrace her love despite looming challenges signal strength of character. This portrayal inspires young readers, advocating resilience in the face of adversity.

Subtle hints of external conflicts emerge, setting the stage for battles yet to come. Readers are poised on the precipice, eager to see how each character will respond to the trials ahead. These symbolic elements enrich the story, adding depth and suspense as the narrative progresses.

In the end, readers will walk away, understanding that love, beautiful and daunting, invites its own set of challenges. Our protagonist's journey, full of twists, turns, and countless lessons, prepares them for their ventures into love and life, armed with the courage and conviction to face whatever comes next.

As the days pass, the weight of hidden glances and whispered conversations takes its toll. What once felt thrilling now wears on her, the joy of their connection mixed with the strain of secrecy. At school, every laugh shared or touch exchanged starts to feel like a gamble. One wrong move, one careless word could expose their hidden world to judgment. She watches him from across the cafeteria, her heart racing as he catches her eye. Their smiles are bright yet tinged with the knowledge of the risks they face. They are two stars in a galaxy that shun their light, each longing to shine more brightly but held back by fear.

Later that evening, she stands in front of her mirror, tracing her fingers along the tiny bracelet he gave her. The silver glints in the soft light of her room, a physical reminder of their bond. She whispers to her reflection, debating whether to share her feelings with her closest friend, Caitlyn. Caitlyn is known for her loyalty, yet the thought of her friend's possible reaction stirs a knot in her stomach. Would Caitlyn understand? Would she think their love is wrong? The room's silence feels heavy as she tries to gather the courage to speak her truth, but hesitation wraps around her voice like a tight fist.

The next day, she meets Caitlyn after school, the golden sunlight filtering through the trees as they settle on a bench in the park. The air is warm, but a chill runs through her. "Can I tell you something?"

she begins, her throat tight. Caitlyn turns, curiosity written on her face. "Of course! What's up?" The words tumble out like a cascade as she describes her feelings, each confession pulling her closer to a release of pent-up fear. Caitlyn listens intently, nodding and biting her lip. As she finishes, waiting for a reaction, uncertainty lingers like a dance between them.

Finally, Caitlyn leans back and lets out a slow breath. "It's okay to feel this way. Love is complicated, especially at our age." Relief sweeps over her, but it's mixed with confusion. "But... what if people don't accept it?" Caitlyn shrugs, a flicker of confidence in her eyes. "They might not. But what's truly important is how you feel. If he makes you happy, that's all that matters." Her friend's encouragement is a shield against the judgmental world outside their bubble. As the sunset paints the sky in hues of orange and pink, hope begins to unfurl within her, a delicate flower fighting against the storm.

However, the relief is short-lived. The following week, rumors swirl, creeping through the halls like a stubborn vine. Whispers of her relationship leak from sources she thought safe. Friendly chatter has shifted to gossip, and suddenly, the world feels much more minor. She catches snippets of conversations that race her heart—"Did you hear about them? It's so scandalous." A cold shiver runs down her spine at the judgment in their voices—her initial spark now flickers, a candle threatened by the wind of disapproval. Every glance from classmates feels scrutinizing, their eyes heavy with the weight of opinions and expectations.

Amid this chaos, her sanctuary becomes the hidden space where she and her crush can be alone. They find solace in forgotten corners of the school, behind the bleachers during gym class, or in empty classrooms after hours. Each meeting becomes a mix of laughter and whispered fears. "Do you think it's that bad?" she asks one afternoon, worry lacing her words. He shrugs, brushing a hand through his hair. "It doesn't feel wrong when I'm with you." His honesty ignites both warmth and turmoil in her heart. They discuss dreams, escape plans, and possibly being together openly someday. Their conversations lie heavy with hope and caution, tethered by the realities of their surroundings.

As the weeks continue, her internal struggle shifts with the rising tension around them. Every instance of laughter is edged with the potential for heartache. She notices the distance growing between her and Caitlyn, who seems unsure how to act around her now. Her friend chats with others, eyes flickering back at her with uncertainty as if gauging the risk of association. It's another layer of complexity that weighs on her, planting seeds of doubt in her mind. Are they too different? Is love strong enough to withstand the pressure of disapproval?

One day, she finds herself alone in the library, surrounded by books that whisper of great romances but feel so distant from her own. She's come to research famous couples who faced adversity, hoping to find guidance. As she turns the pages, she realizes their stories often involve triumph but usually at a significant cost. She feels a wandering eye on her and looks up to find her crush standing at the entrance, looking both eager and anxious. Without a word, he crosses the room and slips into the seat beside her, the world outside forgotten at that moment. She can't help but breathe a little easier. In this miniature sanctuary filled with history, they can carve out a space for their love, free from prying eyes.

"What are you reading?" he asks, glancing at the book in her hands. A smile breaks through her worries as she shows him the cover, launching into a quick summary of a couple who defied the odds. His laughter fills the air, banishing the tension of the outside world, if only for a moment. "So, we just need a grand gesture, right?" he jokes, eyes dancing with mischief. She chuckles, the heaviness in her heart lightening. "Or maybe we just need to be ourselves." Their quiet understanding strengthens their connection, pushing the chaos beyond those library walls further from their minds.

But reality waits, lurking beyond their moments of escape. The following day, she opens her locker to find a note hastily folded and crumpled. "Everyone's talking," it reads. Her stomach drops, the words echoing like thunder. She glances around, suddenly aware of the stares from classmates. Caitlyn stands nearby, watching her intently, perhaps sensing her turmoil. The walls of her tunneled world press in, and the stakes feel higher than ever

CHAPTER 3

Moments of Clarity

In a world that often feels like an unending storm, the journey to understanding love begins with moments of clarity. For many young hearts stepping into the realm of first love, every glance and whispered secret becomes a vibrant thread in the tapestry of their stories. This book invites you into the lives of those navigating this intricate dance—where friendship intertwines with romance, and vulnerability emerges as both a challenge and a gift.

Imagine confiding your deepest secrets to a friend on a rainy afternoon, the sound of raindrops echoing the rhythm of your beating heart. Trust, as simple as it seems, is the foundation upon which our emotional worlds are built. When the protagonist shares their feelings about a new romance, they discover the healing power inherent in revealing one's soul. Within these moments of trust, we find solace, a sanctuary where we can be ourselves without fear of judgment. By allowing themselves to be vulnerable, the protagonist finds support in unexpected places, transforming uncertainty into a shared experience.

Balancing love with friendship brings its unique challenges. As the protagonist dances between the gravitational pull of new romance and the steadfast nature of existing friendships, they begin to appreciate friends' stability amid the whirlwind of emotions. Friends not only provide laughter and comfort but also act as mirrors reflecting our growth. Through countless conversations, from late-night texts to heart-to-heart talks under starlit skies, friendships are lifelines, grounding us when love threatens to sweep us off our feet.

Yet, with love comes risk—a whisper of the forbidden that thrills even as it terrifies. The protagonist's relationship tests societal boundaries, pushing them to consider the weight of external expectations. Every choice carries potential consequences, rippling their personal lives and affecting how others perceive them. In this complicated space, the protagonist confronts the cost of love, weighing joy against potential heartbreak. Here lies the essence of growing up: understanding the delicate dance of decision-making and its impact on family dynamics and self-identity.

Friendships, too, are tested, revealing the complex web of emotions activated by new romantic pursuits. Protective glances and cautious words from friends create a tension that demands careful navigation. How does one pursue love without losing cherished connections? By learning to set and communicate boundaries, the protagonist begins to protect these relationships while following their heart's desires.

One of the most profound revelations on this journey is witnessing another person's vulnerability. In glimpsing the hidden battles faced by their lover, the protagonist realizes the transformative power of empathy. Understanding that everyone carries unseen scars fosters compassion and strengthens their bond. These moments become touchstones, deepening their connection as they share experiences rooted in pain and healing. Together, they build a safe space where honesty flourishes, creating an intimacy forged in shared vulnerabilities.

Sharing stories—those illuminating tales of past struggles—becomes a balm for both souls involved. Storytelling isn't just an exchange of words but a path toward mutual understanding and acceptance. As the protagonist listens, they find pieces of themselves mirrored back in their partner's narrative, affirming their journey and igniting a spark of hope for healing.

Amidst the chaos, the importance of self-awareness comes sharply into focus. The protagonist learns to articulate their swirling emotions, crafting a clearer sense of identity. Self-awareness encourages open conversations, helping the protagonist understand what they seek in this turbulent sea of emotions. Setting personal boundaries emerges as an essential act of self-preservation, empowering them to grow even as love reshapes their world.

Reflecting on one's desires, fears, and needs can illuminate paths otherwise shrouded in doubt. Through introspection, the protagonist discovers lurking doubts and unvoiced dreams, gaining insights that guide them toward happiness. Embracing uncertainty and recognizing it as a natural companion on the voyage of love becomes an invaluable lesson. By accepting unpredictability, the protagonist uncovers resilience within themselves and learn that beauty often hides in the chaotic dance of evolving relationships.

As you delve into this book, remember that the stories woven within are more than mere narratives; they are reflections of real journeys—the highs and lows, the laughter and tears, and the quiet moments of clarity that shape us. Love does not exist in isolation; it is a complex tapestry interwoven with friendship, vulnerability, and self-discovery. Here, young adults will find echoes of their own experiences, exploring what it means to navigate first love in a world teetering between destruction and rebirth.

For those seeking tales of personal growth and healing, this book invites them to join the protagonist on their journey. You will uncover lessons in expressing emotions, recognizing risks, and embracing vulnerability—all vital in fostering meaningful connections that can withstand the tests of time. And perhaps, amidst these pages, you will find your moments of clarity guiding you toward a deeper understanding of yourself and the extraordinary people who touch your life.

Amidst the shifting tides of adolescence, the protagonist discovers that friendships evolve alongside romantic relationships. One sunny afternoon, they meet with their best friend, Mia, at their favorite coffee shop. "You've been distant lately. What's going on?" Mia's voice cuts through the chatter around them. The open concern in her eyes tugs at the protagonist's heartstrings. They take a deep breath, contemplating how to share the whirlwind of emotions they're grappling with. "I've just been... you know, figuring some stuff out with Jason." Mia leans in, her curiosity piqued. "Jason? The guy you've been talking about? What's the deal?" This seated conversation feels grounding, a reminder of friendship's stability amid the storm of budding romance.

In the warm light filtering through the window, the protagonist reveals moments spent with Jason—his laughter, the way his eyes spark when he talks about his passions and those quiet, tender hugs that feel like home. Mia listens intently, nodding along with a smile. "He seems great! But are you really in this for the right reasons?" The gentle probing catches the protagonist off guard. It's easy to lose sight of intentions when everything feels perfectly chaotic. "I think so. It's just... I'm scared," the protagonist admits. The weight of fear lingers in the air, heavy and familiar. Mia's hand reaches across the table, offering support. "Fear is normal. But don't forget to check in with yourself. Are you being true to yourself?"

With those words, the protagonist revisits their journey, examining the edges of their own heart. Yet, confusion looms like clouds overhead. The novel's complexity of emotions leaves them wondering if their feelings for Jason are real or a fantasy painted by the allure of first love. A flicker of doubt surfaces; is this spark real enough to withstand the storms they're witnessing among their friends, too? Conversations swirl, friends adapt to new dynamics, and jealousy nips at the edges, knocking on the doors of their secure bubble. Sensing the turmoil, Mia knows it's essential for the protagonist to find clarity in these moments. "What do you want?" she asks gently, giving space for introspection.

The protagonist stares at the swirling patterns in their coffee. "I want to feel safe. But... I also don't want to lose Jason. What if I become too much, and he walks away?" The sigh escapes, laced with vulnerability. Friends share advice like lifelines but also bring the weight of expectations. "Just remember, if he can't handle you at your most vulnerable, is he the one?" Mia's words carry the strength of truth, nudging the protagonist toward self-discovery. They begin to grasp that navigating love means navigating self-love.

Days slip by, enveloped in the colors of brewing emotions. The protagonist finds the courage to communicate her intentions clearly with Jason. "Hey, can we talk about what this means for us?" they ask, heart racing and fidgeting with their hands during an evening stroll at the park. Jason stops, the sunlight glinting off his hair, his expression softening. "Of course. I've sensed something's been bothering you." Relief washes over the protagonist. It's a treasured moment—an opening to share joys and fears.

As they converse, the protagonist shares everything—insecurities, excitement, the vast tapestry of their budding relationship, and even the doubts lingering in their mind. "I really like you, Jason," they confess, vulnerability blooming like the flowers lining the pathway. "But I'm scared of losing myself if we rush into this." Jason offers a soft smile, brushing a hand through his hair. "I get it. But we can take our time. I like you for you, not some version you think I want." The assurance echoes in the protagonist's heart, filling it with warmth and relief.

Through these conversations, they discover the balance of communication and authenticity, the lifeblood of any relationship. Nights spent laughing and sharing dreams blend into quiet afternoons, where words sometimes elude them, and comfortable silence reigns instead. The protagonist learns to navigate the realms of being present in both love and friendship—a tightrope walk between worlds that now intersect in such beautiful ways.

Yet, not everything is smooth sailing. As their connection deepens with Jason, the protagonist begins to distance themselves from friends, causing a rift they hadn't anticipated. One evening, as laughter fills the air during a group outing, jealousy creeps in when Mia sidesteps them, her playful banter reserved. The protagonist catches the subtle shift and approaches, concern lining their face. "Mia, are you okay? You seem... off." The question lingers heavily, an unspoken awareness emerging between them.

"I'm fine!" Mia replies a bit too sharply. "It's just hard seeing you with him so much." An uncomfortable silence descends. "I thought we were all in this together," the protagonist stutters, frustration bubbling. Emotions spill over, igniting the seams of the friendship. "We are! But it feels like you're changing!" The truth stings; the words pierced both their hearts. "Maybe I'm just trying to find a balance," the protagonist counters, hoping to mend the fractures opening up.

Words tumble, raw and unfiltered. Addressing feelings rather than sweeping them under the carpet becomes a lesson in its own right. As they navigate this turmoil, each emotion shared chips away at solitude, slowly leading them toward a mutual understanding of love, friendship, and their place in their co-writing narrative.

The protagonist realizes this can be an opportunity rather than an impasse: to explore how love can coexist with friendship. They reach out through text later that week, an olive branch offered amid the tumult. "Let's hang out. Just us." With shared efforts, they can begin to mend, stitching together the tapestry of their lives with gratitude and patience—a realization that bonds can withstand the tests of change.

In the country of young hearts, resilience blooms alongside budding romance, and small victories echo dances through crowded hallways, turning uncertainties into accidental joy. Each step, whether a misstep or stride, brings them closer to understanding the delicate art of balancing love with the roots of friendship. The protagonist embraces the roller coaster, ready to ride the waves of growth unerringly, even as the storms of youth linger beyond their view.

CHAPTER 4

Hidden Cracks

In the tangled tapestry of teenage life, where emotions run high and every moment feels amplified, love and heartbreak become defining chapters in our personal stories. For young adults stepping into this world, these experiences are both exhilarating and terrifying. They are the moments that light up our souls yet sometimes threaten to burn us with their intensity. This book delves into those powerful feelings, offering a narrative that resonates with anyone who has ever navigated the rollercoaster of first love and the inevitable cracks it may unveil in our emotional armor.

Our protagonist is a young woman who seems to have it all together—or at least that is what she wants everyone to believe. Surrounded by friends and admirers, she is far from alone, yet beneath her confident exterior lies a different reality. This story peels back the layers to reveal hidden struggles, exploring how past wounds shape her present relationships and her burgeoning romance. It explores vulnerability, which emerges as a profound strength capable of forging genuine connections rather than being considered a weakness.

From an early age, our protagonist learned about expectations. Family and peers held certain ideals over her head like unreachable stars, casting shadows of inadequacy across her self-image. These expectations whispered that she must be perfect and that anything less was not enough. As she ventures into her first serious relationship, these whispers become deafening, feeding a nagging doubt that she can never truly meet anyone's standards—including her own. The weight of this pressure complicates her budding love as fears of not being enough persistently shadowed her happiness.

Life's silent burdens are another of her companions. Her past is sprinkled with instances of abandonment and loss, leaving scars that haven't healed but instead have transformed into walls built around her heart. The fear that letting someone in will only lead to pain makes trust elusive. Her relationship falters as she oscillates between desire and the haunting belief that deep love invites inevitable sorrow. Encountering a new love interest sparks both hope and apprehension, stirring old memories while offering the chance for something meaningful.

Despite her social circle, an intrinsic loneliness pervades her life. She could be surrounded by laughter and chatter yet feel completely disconnected—like an outsider looking in. This internal solitude prompts her to hide her genuine emotions, afraid of judgment or misunderstanding. Authentic connections seem to slip away as she questions her worthiness for love. Her public facade of vibrancy is starkly contrasted by her private struggles, magnifying her inner conflict.

A journey toward self-awareness begins almost imperceptibly. Subtle cues in her interactions signal a need to address her past influences. Realization dawns one day as if a fog is lifting, revealing the patterns that dictate her actions. Past trauma has left its fingerprint on her life, and acknowledging this becomes crucial. That moment of clarity serves as a catalyst, setting the stage for a more profound understanding of her love interest. It begins a healing process and lays the groundwork for genuine intimacy.

The realization that past pains still weave through her present is liberating. Sharing these insights with her partner initiates the healing journey. By confronting these traumas openly, she discovers that vulnerability, once feared, is transformative. It turns out to be an act of courage, inviting mutual trust rather than rejection. Her openness sets an example for others living similar stories, illuminating the path to healing.

Dialogue plays an essential role in unpacking emotional baggage. Conversations create bridges, turning silent suffering into shared understanding. Through her stories, empathy blossoms—not just from her partner but also within herself, where acceptance grows. This exchange normalizes their experiences and fears, knitting them closer together. Their dialogue reveals overlapping backgrounds and reinforces the message that they are not alone on their emotional journey.

Their connection thrives on collective scars, uncovering mutual pain that deepens their bond. Knowing they share a history of hurt fosters empathy and respect, paving a pathway to healing. Vulnerability, now seen in a new light, highlights the strength of embracing emotional truth. Through this lens, it becomes clear that opening up emotionally fortifies their relationship more than any pretense of perfection ever could.

Establishing safety becomes pivotal as they navigate their evolving relationship. A haven is crafted where emotions are welcomed without judgment—a sanctuary of belonging and acceptance. Both partners learn to accept their flaws, moving beyond fears of rejection to embrace authenticity. Trust builds gradually, with each moment of openness becoming a thread weaving their lives more closely together.

This narrative aims to show readers that acknowledging emotional scars is not merely cathartic but foundational for creating meaningful bonds. Vulnerability is revealed as a bridge rather than a chasm, emphasizing its vital role in nurturing trust and intimacy. Readers are invited to explore their vulnerabilities through the protagonist's journey and discover how such introspection might enhance their relationships.

So, dear reader, accompany our protagonist as she grapples with insecurities, learns the art of vulnerability, and ultimately finds strength in her scars. Here lies a story of growth—where uncovering hidden cracks doesn't signify brokenness but rather the magnificent beginnings of real love forged in honesty and acceptance.

Their first conversation about the future happened during a quiet afternoon, sitting on the grass outside the school. The sun cast warm shadows, creating a sense of peace that was hard to find in their whirlwind lives. "What do you see for yourself in a couple of years?" he asked, tilting his head toward her. She hesitated, taking in the question as if it were a foreign language. "I guess... I hope to be happy," she finally replied, fidgeting with a stray blade of grass. "But sometimes I worry I won't be enough, you know?"

He nodded, understanding flooding his expression. "You're not defined by what you achieve. You're already enough just being you." She looked at him with wide eyes, sensing the sincerity in his words. "But what if you feel like you have to prove something? What if the world expects more?" There was a moment of silence, the weight of her fears hanging in the air.

"I get that," he said slowly. "But it's not about proving anything to others. It's about what makes you feel fulfilled. You need to follow your path, not the one everyone else lays out for you." A flicker of hope ignited within her. Could it be as simple as believing in her worth? That conversation was a turning point, prompting her to reflect on what mattered.

Days turned into weeks, and their bond deepened with every shared secret and laugh. They began attending art classes together; it was a space where she could express herself freely, away from the clutches of expectations. One evening, as they smeared paint on canvases, she saw his focused expression. "What are you thinking about?" she asked, curious. "Just how color can change everything," he replied, dipping his brush into a vibrant hue. "And we're all a mix of different colors, right?"

His metaphor hit home. "Yeah, I guess I never thought of it that way," she admitted. "Sometimes, I feel like just a washed-out gray in a world full of bright colors." He turned towards her, eyes locking on hers. "You're not gray. You're a beautiful shade, even if you can't see it yet." The sincerity in his voice made her heart flutter. As they painted side by side, laughter filled the air, washing away remnants of self-doubt.

However, street corners and coffee shop booths couldn't forever shield her from the outside world. At school, whispers followed her around like shadows. One afternoon, as she exited the art room, she overheard a couple of classmates giggling, mentioning her name. "Did you see how desperate she is? It's like she's clinging to him for validation." The words stung, raw, and painful.

She confronted him later that day, fear gripping her heart tightly. "What if they're right? What if I am using you to fill some void?" The unease twisted in her stomach as she spoke, desperately seeking confirmation that he saw her for who she was. "If they're talking about us, it means whatever we have is more important than they can understand," he said, his tone firm yet understanding. "You aren't a reflection of their judgments. You're so much more."

A quiet resolve settled within her. His belief in her was becoming a lifeline. Dealing with external pressures, she found herself turning inward more frequently. Late-night talks grew deeper, swapping dreams under a blanket of stars. "What happened with us feels real," he once said, his voice low. "It's like I can be my true self without any mask."

Her heart warmed at his admission. "Same. I've never felt more at home with anyone before." The gentle breeze danced around them, carrying their words and laughter into the universe. But those moments of happiness she was brushed up against an unsettling truth: the past never entirely dissipated.

One evening, over pizza at their favorite spot, he posed a question that made her pause. "What scares you the most about us?" She looked away, chewing on her lip, feeling the weight of his gaze on her. "I think... it's losing you," she finally whispered, vulnerability creeping into her voice. "What if I mess it up because of my past?"

His expression softened, reaching across the table to take her hand. "We all carry baggage. What matters is that we face it together. You don't need to run from it." She absorbed his words, feeling both terrified and relieved. It was a revelation—facing her fears instead of hiding from them.

In the following days, she embarked on a new chapter of honesty. Therapy would help her unpack the multitude of emotions she had shoved deep down, so she decided to seek support. "I think talking to someone could help me," she told him as they walked through a park. "Maybe understanding my feelings can clear some of the fog."

His smile radiated warmth. "I think that's a great idea. Taking steps to heal is brave." The support anchored her as she took tentative steps toward understanding herself. Her sessions unveiled layers of feelings—the grief and fear driving her actions. Each breakthrough was both exhilarating and daunting, but it was also freeing.

Their relationship matured; actions replaced words. Sitting in his room one rainy afternoon, she found comfort in silence as they painted in their bubbles. The world outside blurred, but inside, she felt whole. "I never imagined this would be my reality," she said softly without looking up.

He smiled, and brush paused mid-air. "It's just the beginning. There's so much more to explore." The simplicity of their connection was a reminder that real love thrived not in grand gestures but in quiet moments shared amidst the chaos of life. Searching for her inner strength brought a fresh resolve to their relationship.

Their conversations took on newfound gravity as she processed her emotions, revealing uncharted territories. Topics shifted from mere concerns about the future to dreams buried beneath layers of fear. With every shared experience, she unknotted the strings, tying her past to a present that could finally breathe.

But with growth often comes resistance. Doubts resurfaced—moments when insecurities crept back in, whispering their toxic narratives. "What if this is just a phase?" she wondered aloud one night, turning the question over like a worn-out coin.

"Even if it is," he responded gently, "it's still worth having right now. And, regardless of what happens later, today is real." She leaned back, letting the truth settle like a comforting blanket. For the first time in her life, she felt the weight of the past begin to lift.

CHAPTER 5

Forbidden Echoes

In life's journey, few experiences strike as profoundly as the first taste of love. It's a time of discovery and excitement as if stepping into a world that is both familiar and foreign—a realm where emotions run high and every glance or whisper feels laden with meaning. For young adults poised at this threshold, grappling with the intricate dance between desire and expectation, love often comes as both a blessing and a trial.

Our story begins amidst these tangled feelings, centered on a protagonist whose heart beats fiercely against the backdrop of conventional norms. She is a young woman caught in the tidal pull of forbidden love, a love that stirs up friction in her world. While her heart seeks connection and understanding, the world around her seems determined to scrutinize her every move.

For her, family isn't just a foundation but a fortress, with walls built from generations of tradition. These walls dictate whom she should love—and, more significantly, whom she shouldn't. In this labyrinthine tangle of cultural expectations lies the challenge: balancing what feels innately right against what has been prescribed by those she loves most. Her family, though acting out of a desire to protect and guide, inadvertently becomes an obstacle, erecting barriers invisible to them but all too tangible for her.

Every conversation at the dinner table seems like a veiled negotiation, a coded language for her to decipher. Hidden beneath polite discussions about education and prospects are the unspoken rules that press her to conform. The weight of their expectations seeps into her daily life, affecting decisions big and small, sowing seeds of doubt as she questions her path. This inner turmoil only deepens as arguments erupt over the legitimacy of her love, leaving behind emotional scars etched with angry words that hint at disappointment and betrayal.

The dilemma of love versus duty weighs heavily on our protagonist's shoulders. Torn between filial piety and her own heart, she navigates a world inclined to judge rather than understand. Family gatherings, once simple affairs full of warmth, now seem laced with underlying tension, each interaction a reminder of the widening chasm between her desires and her responsibilities.

Yet, within the confines of this struggle lies a space for introspection—a moment when she can confront her fears and ambitions. Here, she reflects on how much of herself belongs to her family and what part remains independent, free to follow its rhythm. Through this reflection, readers are invited to ponder their beliefs and question how societal expectations shape who they are and what they value.

Beyond family, another layer of complexity emerges—her peers. As supportive as friends might initially appear, the harsh truth of gossip and rumor quickly reveals itself. Idle chatter becomes a storm, chipping away at her self-image and portraying a distorted reality. Social gatherings morph into trials where whispered judgments and sidelong glances challenge her resolve.

Feelings of isolation grow as friendships, once thought sturdy, begin to falter, strained by misunderstandings and shifting allegiances. She must navigate this ever-changing landscape, learning to discern genuine support from superficial acceptance. The quest for solidarity becomes a journey not just alongside friends but also within herself, discovering resilience amidst chaos.

Inevitably, the outside world's pressure culminates in a public confrontation, a pivotal moment where everything hangs in the balance. Picture the scene: a crowded place buzzing with people, voices rising and falling like waves crashing against rocks. Tension electrifies the air as eyes focus on her, waiting for the drama to unfold. It's a moment when time slows, allowing every emotion to surface—fear, frustration, defiance.

Her voice, though trembling, holds a steely resolve as she stands firm, articulating her feelings for all to hear. Supportive murmurs intermix with critical jeers from onlookers, creating a cacophony. Her love interest, steadfast by her side, offers silent strength, grounding her amidst the tumult. Together, they present a unified front against the disapproving backdrop, challenging societal norms one courageous step at a time.

This confrontation creates a chance for growth—not just in their relationship but also within our protagonist's heart. In facing public scrutiny, she embarks on a journey of self-discovery, redefining what love means in the context of her life. No longer constrained by external dictates, she embraces a vision of love that is personal yet strong, forged through trials.

Learning to create safe spaces becomes integral to nurturing their bond, offering solace from the outside world. In private moments shared away from prying eyes, their connection deepens, unfettered by judgment. Love transforms into a sanctuary, a refuge where joy and healing coexist, nurturing their souls.

Through conversations imbued with honesty and compromise, they find common ground, navigating the imperfections inherent in any relationship. Together, they embrace the idea that love, while layered and sometimes painful, is ultimately worth pursuing. It's not about perfection but rather about patience, understanding, and the willingness to adapt as they walk hand in hand toward an uncertain future.

As this story unfolds, it reflects the real-world struggles of many young people who seek to define love on their own terms. Readers journey alongside the protagonist, gaining insights into the complexities of relationships and emerging with a renewed appreciation for the beauty found in love's many forms.

In the aftermath of the confrontation, our protagonist reflects on the mixed reactions she received. Some faces in the crowd showed sympathy; others revealed disdain. On the walk home, she glances at her love interest, now more vital to her than ever. "Did you see their faces?" she asks, half in disbelief and amused. He nods, a small smile breaking through his solemnity. "Yeah, but we're stronger than their opinions." This moment, filled with unspoken agreement, begins to weave a new thread into the fabric of their story, one that they can explore together away from judgment.

As days pass, her resolve solidifies, but insecurities linger like shadows. She holds her head high at school, but whispers still curl around her like smoke. In art class, she sits with friends too consumed with their own lives to notice her struggle. She sketches, allowing her emotions to flow onto the paper, the softness of the charcoal contrasting with her hardening heart. "What are you drawing?" her friend Amy leans over, a curious glint in her eye. "Just thoughts," she replies, not wanting to divulge too much. Amy shrugs, returning to her project, oblivious to the silent storm within her friend.

Later that evening, she discusses the sketch with her love interest over coffee at a cozy café. "It felt good to release those feelings, but it also showed me how much I have to deal with," she shares, momentarily pushing her coffee cup away. He listens intently, his eyes never leaving hers. "You're brave for sharing. They'll learn to respect you," he reassures her. "But what if they don't?" she questions, uncertain. "Then we create our own space. You and me," he responds, his voice steady, instilling a sense of hope in her heart.

Their conversations evolve into deeper discussions about their dreams and fears. Sitting on the café's quaint patio, they forge plans about an uncertain yet exciting future. "What if we traveled together after graduation?" he suggests one afternoon, a spark lighting his eyes. "Away from all this." She leans in, excitement bubbling up within her. "I'd love that! A fresh start, just us." They dive into envisioning their travels, fabricating stories and adventures that stretch across distant landscapes. This dreaming catalyzes their commitment, knitting together their aspirations into a shared tapestry of possibilities.

Amidst this newfound bond, external pressures don't fade; instead, they shift. Conversations at home grow sharper, each comment a jab at the perceived tension between duty and desire. "You have to focus on school, not distractions," her mother insists one evening over dinner, fingers tightly gripping her fork. Her heart sinks. She knows her love for him isn't a distraction. "It's my choice," she responds softly, met with her mother's disappointed gaze. "You think you know best, but these things aren't simple." The word "simple" hangs heavy in the air, and she wishes for the courage to explain the complexities of her heart.

Weeks turn into months, and the seasons change around them. As spring blossoms, the world comes alive, symbolizing the growth within her. She continues to create, pouring her heart into each brushstroke, each piece echoing the duality of her existence. In the warmth of daylight, she navigates friendships with newfound clarity, letting go of those who do not uplift her spirit. The group she once felt tethered to begins to drift, replaced by a new circle around understanding and acceptance. Together, they explore the city, visit galleries, and lose themselves in laughter, sharing the joy of connection, realizing that not all bonds are meant to last forever.

Still, remnants of her past linger like echoes. "It's hard, letting go," she confides to her love interest one evening while they sit on a bench overlooking a sunset-streaked sky. "I feel like I'm losing part of myself." He takes a deep breath, contemplating her words. "You're not losing anything; you're evolving. It's okay to grow apart from things that don't nourish your soul." His gentle insight illuminates her understanding, and she acknowledges the truth in his statement. They sit together in silence, the vibrant colors above mirroring the flames of their new and old connections.

Encounters with family still stir anxiety within her. She often imagines awkward conversation warnings that scrape against her heart. One quiet Sunday, she decides to take the plunge while preparing for dinner. "Mom, can we talk?" Her mother looks up, a mix of concern and hope in her eyes. "Of course, sweetie." With trembling words, she delves into her feelings about the constraints of love and duty, her heart racing. "I want to make choices for myself. It's not easy, but I need you to understand." There's a long pause as her mother absorbs the words, the air thick with unspoken fears and love. "I just want what's best for you," her mother murmurs. "But I see you're fighting for this. We both might need time." They share a fragile but hopeful smile, recognizing this as a step forward.

Slowly, the dynamics within her home begin to change. While the conversations remain challenging, the willingness to engage opens a pathway for reconciliation. Their discussions shift from rigid expectations to a realization that love can exist in many forms, evolving beyond traditional confines. Over shared meals, they find moments of laughter, debate, and reflection—a testament to the slowly bridging chasm that once felt insurmountable. Each dinner becomes a tapestry woven with threads of compromise and understanding, hinting that perhaps love can transcend even the deepest divides.

This metamorphosis reverberates through every facet of her life, knitting together friendships and family ties alike. As she walks alongside her love interest, hand in hand, they refuse to let the outside world dictate their bond. Laughter echoes around them as they share dreams of the future and their shared journey—the record of love etched into every scar, joy, and hope they nurture together.

CHAPTER 6

In the Shadows of Doubt

In the quiet corners of adolescence, love often tiptoes in, unannounced and enigmatic. For young hearts navigating these first turbulent waves, understanding emotions can feel like solving a riddle where the clues are hidden deep within. This book opens its pages to those standing on the precipice of love and heartbreak, inviting them into a world of characters who echo their vulnerabilities and dreams.

Our story unfolds with an unnamed protagonist—let's call her Emma—who finds herself tangled in a web woven from the silken threads of young love. It's a love that promises warmth and storms, carrying whispers of doubt that occasionally shadow the sunshine. As readers, you will step into Emma's shoes, feeling the ground tremble beneath her feet as she walks through the meandering paths of affection, uncertainty, and discovery.

Emma's journey is punctuated by the arrival of someone new: a mysterious stranger whose presence is magnetic yet unsettling. Imagine the thrill of meeting someone who seems to hold the universe within their eyes—a canvas painted with colors you've never seen before. Yet, rather than basking solely in fascination, Emma wrestles with an unexpected adversary: jealousy. It creeps up quietly, making her question her worthiness and casting shadows on her confidence. We all know how tiny sparks of insecurity can ignite emotional wildfires, leading us down unintended roads of assumption and apprehension.

This narrative doesn't avoid confronting the silent battles many of us wage against ourselves. Through Emma's eyes, you will see how misunderstandings can blossom from the smallest seeds—a glance misinterpreted, a moment too quiet—fostering narratives in our minds that veer far from reality. Young love, although exhilarating, is often entangled with such moments of confusion; here, the importance of communication becomes not just a lesson but a lifeline.

Picture a scene where words spill out during a heated exchange fueled by fear and desire. In these intense conversations, relationships face their most significant tests. Emma's vulnerability in these times will draw you closer, showing how easy it is for love to teeter on the edge when we let suspicion overshadow trust. In these fiery moments, the need for openness shines through the haze, illuminating paths toward healing.

Amidst the chaos, Emma finds solace in self-reflection. Her journal becomes a sanctuary where thoughts untangle, and truths emerge. Writing provides clarity, revealing unspoken insecurities and helping her understand the roots of her jealousy. It's a powerful reminder of the importance of turning inward, allowing young readers to relate to the messy, often chaotic process of deciphering feelings and finding peace within themselves.

Doubt, however, is relentless. It persists, lurking in Emma's mind like an unwelcome guest, prompting her to question the intentions of those around her. Here lies the complex tension between hope and skepticism—an eternal dance experienced by many stepping into love's arena. As mysterious as he is charming, the stranger sends mixed signals, leaving Emma confused. How often have we all stood at the crossroads of what we perceive and what indeed is, battling the internal storms they conjure?

Friends offer both refuge and challenge. Their advice, while well-meaning, adds layers to Emma's uncertainty—a familiar dilemma for anyone torn between outside perceptions and personal judgments. This external pressure captures the essence of societal expectations, reminding readers that the path to understanding oneself is rarely linear.

Emma confronts the stranger in a pivotal moment, bearing her concerns and fears. It's a brave leap toward transparency—a testament to the courage needed to build bridges of understanding amidst swirling doubts. This confrontation isn't just about seeking answers but embracing vulnerability, a quality essential for any meaningful connection.

Through honest dialogue, revelations surface, soothing the tempest within Emma's heart. Trust begins to mend the frayed edges of their relationship. In this narrative twist, readers witness the transformative power of truth, reinforcing the message that love, at its core, flourishes in the light of honesty.

Beyond the realm of romance, Emma grapples with a more profound conflict: the battle with her self-worth. Against the backdrop of peers seemingly more confident and more beautiful, her journey reflects the universal struggle against comparison. Readers glimpse the tender process of learning to value oneself amidst external pressures—a journey toward embracing imperfections and nurturing self-love.

Support arrives unexpectedly, cloaked in the wisdom of an elder or the candid insights shared within an online community. These unconventional guides nudge Emma toward self-discovery, illustrating how guidance often emerges from places we least anticipate. The realization that wisdom can be gleaned from diverse experiences encourages readers to seek insight beyond traditional avenues, enriching their quests for understanding.

As Emma navigates through these emotional landscapes, the book stitches together growth, resilience, and healing stories. It gently reminds readers that, despite the challenges, there lies immense beauty in the journey itself. Each chapter unfolds with lessons learned, encouraging young adults—and anyone who has ever loved—to confront their fears, embrace their flaws, and find strength in vulnerability.

Much like the rest of the story, this introduction aims to resonate deeply with hearts open to exploration. Welcome to a tale where love mirrors life, and every page turned offers a beacon of hope, guiding you through your experiences of love, doubt, and eventual clarity.

Emma sits on her bed, the journal resting on her lap, its pages slightly worn from her constant scribbles. She pauses, reflecting on the words she had written the night before. "You can't let fear control you," she had written. It echoed loudly in her mind, prompting her to take a deep breath. She thinks about her friends and how they each wear their masks. "Do you think he likes me?" she asks her best friend Mia during lunch, her voice barely concealing the quiver of uncertainty. "Of course! He does. Just look at how he looks at you!" Mia replies with an excitement that almost feels like a warm hug. But Emma isn't convinced. The hints of jealousy linger like a ghost hovering over her heart.

The next day brings a surprise. The stranger, whose name she learns is Lucas, approaches her in the school hallway, brushing his fingers through his messy hair. "Hey, Emma. Want to grab coffee after school?" he asks casually, his tone light yet inviting. Emma's heart races, a blend of eagerness and doubt crashing within her. "Uh, sure. That sounds nice," she responds, the corners of her mouth curving into a cautious smile. As she walks away, she whispers, "What does this mean? Is it just coffee or something more?" Her mind races with scenarios, each more elaborate than the last, weaving doubt into excitement.

That day rolls by painfully slowly. She can hardly focus in math class, flipping through her notes but retaining none of the information. Each time she glances at Lucas, a few rows ahead, she feels a fluttering mixture of excitement and anxiety. When the bell finally rings, Emma rushes out, her heart pounding with anticipation. The aroma envelops her as she reaches the coffee shop, calming her nerves slightly. Lucas stands near the entrance, a grin on his face as he spots her. "Right on time," he says, his voice smooth and self-assured. "I hope you like this place."

Over coffee, they dive into an easy, flowing conversation. Lucas shares stories about his family, and Emma talks about her obsession with reading. There's laughter, shared smiles, and the fleeting touches of fingers reaching for the same muffin. Emma feels warmth flooding her, yet doubt lingers like an unsettling shadow. "What if I'm not enough for him?" she thinks, biting her lower lip. Lucas's voice breaks her thoughts. "There's a book I think you would love. It's about learning to accept who you are." Emma meets his gaze, surprised and intrigued. "What's it called?" she asks, her heart slightly lighter.

As their connection deepens over coffee, Emma's anxiety drifts away. They move to a park nearby, sitting on a bench under sprawling trees, the evening golden with the glow of sunset. "I've been meaning to ask," Lucas begins, his tone shifting to something more serious. "What do you really want in a relationship?" Emma blinks, caught off guard by the directness of the question. She hesitates, gathering her thoughts. "I guess... honesty," she replies slowly. "I want to be able to talk without fear of judgment." Lucas nods, his eyes searching hers, inviting more. "And that's what I want," he assures her. Somehow, his sincerity feels like a balm.

Just as the conversation unfolds into deeper territories, Emma's phone buzzes. It's Mia sending a video, capturing moments at a party. Emma's heart sinks at the sight of others—smiling faces, lively dances, and laughter echoing in the background. "Are you going to the party tonight?" Lucas asks, tilting his head slightly. Emma hesitates, the tightness in her chest returning. "I don't know. I wasn't invited." Lucas raises an eyebrow, his expression shifting to concern. "It's just a gathering among friends. You should come if you want to." His words hang in the air, challenging her to step beyond her comfort zone.

Emma arrives at the party after a week of tangled emotions, her heart racing again. It's packed; music thumps against her chest like a second heartbeat. Amidst the laughter and chatter, she feels small and unsure of her place. But then, she spots Lucas across the room. He catches her eye and grins, beckoning her over. "I'm glad you made it," he says, his voice warm amidst the chaos. Emma breathes a sigh of relief, feeling welcomed in his presence. They dance like the only two in the crowded room, sharing easy smiles and fleeting touches.

Suddenly, Mia approaches, her eyes glinting with curiosity. "Are you two dating now?" she asks, grinning widely. Emma blushes, caught off guard by the directness. She glances at Lucas, who shrugs with a playful smirk. "I hope so. I mean, I wouldn't mind," he chimes in, his voice light and teasing. Emma feels her heart soar, uncertainty momentarily lifting.

Emma twirls playfully as the music shifts to a new, familiar, and upbeat song. Lucas catches her, their laughter blending with the rhythm. Each moment spills into the next—a mix of joy and confusion. But then, the door swings open. Another girl enters—a classmate known for her confidence and beauty. Emma's smile falters for just a second. Lucas's attention shifts briefly, and Emma's heart drops into her stomach. Perhaps her fears were justified. Doubts swirl like autumn leaves caught in a breeze, making her question everything again.

"Don't let her get to you," Emma whispers to herself, but her resolve begins to fray. She takes a deep breath, reminding herself to focus on the moment, to let the music drown out the anxiety. The party proceeds, each moment tinged with uncertainty—but also potential. Connections spark around her, friendships deepen, and laughter grows louder. Emma clings to Lucas, who draws her into an embrace on the edge of the room, shielding her beneath the bright lights. Together, they savor the fleeting moments, yet the whispers of jealousy echo at the back of Emma's mind, refusing to settle.

CHAPTER 7

Finding Resilience

In a world where every heartbeat feels like an echo of your own, navigating the first experiences of love and heartbreak can seem overwhelming. It's as if you're suddenly thrust into a maze, trying to find your way while grappling with both exhilarating and bewildering emotions. These feelings are integral to the journey of young adults, shaping personal growth and understanding. This book is a companion on this path, offering solace and insight for those seeking stories that reflect the challenges and triumphs inherent in such emotional journeys.

Amid this whirlwind of emotions lies a seldom-discussed strength: resilience. Finding resilience may seem daunting in the realm of heartbreak; however, clarity and self-discovery emerge precisely during these moments of chaos. Imagine feeling lost and disoriented, like a ship adrift on a turbulent sea. Even in disarray, the determination to regroup and rebuild beckons us forward, fueled by the realization that clarity often arises from the chaos we yearn to escape. Young hearts may relate deeply to being cast into unfamiliar waters, disconnected from their previous selves. However, acknowledging this turmoil becomes vital to finding resilience and eventually attaining peace.

Heartbreak is heavy; it bears down upon us with a weight that permeates daily life, transforming the mundane into something monumental. Recognizing this emotional burden and facing it head-on paves the way for healing. It's okay to feel lost because these emotions initiate a profound journey that demands vulnerability and the shedding of societal stigmas attached to emotional openness. Through small, actionable steps, one can reclaim fragments of joy and rediscover a commitment to growth. Hope rekindles in these modest beginnings, demonstrating how even the faintest glimmer of determination can illuminate the darkest paths.

Reflecting on past experiences offers crucial insights and guides present and future growth. Individuals cultivate resilience and fortify their foundations by drawing lessons from the tapestry of heartbreak they endure. Self-reflection unveils layers of personal understanding, encouraging readers to perceive heartbreak not just as a painful event but as a transformative teacher imparting invaluable wisdom.

Reclaiming independence is another pivotal chapter in this narrative as individuals journey to redefine self-worth and embrace autonomy post-heartbreak. Relationships do not define who we are; instead, they complement the richness of our identities. Emphasizing self-love and respect lays the groundwork for healthy connections, urging readers to cherish their individuality despite external pressures. This newfound independence fosters personal growth, providing clarity and direction in future relationships. The protagonist in our tale explores new passions and interests, discovering that such pursuits serve as healing therapies and avenues for creative self-expression. Engaging with what sparks joy nurtures the soul, reinforcing the power of pursuing one's passions.

Establishing healthy boundaries emerges as a cornerstone of self-preservation; learning to assert needs without hesitation is an empowering exercise. Examples from the protagonist's journey illustrate how clearly defined boundaries translate into robust and healthier relationships. Personal agency becomes intertwined with self-respect as independence flourishes. Reflecting on past and current relationships allows for critical assessment, identifying patterns that compromise self-identity versus those that nurture growth. Understanding these dynamics further entrenches the narrative of autonomy and personal evolution.

Confidence grows steadily through small victories—a theme vividly depicted through the protagonist's incremental achievements. Celebrating minor accomplishments reinstates self-belief, marking each brave act as a stepping stone toward empowerment. Acknowledging progress reinforces confidence and reminds us of the profound impact of small actions on overall well-being.

Facing fears head-on requires bravery, a quality evident when stepping beyond comfort zones leads to revelations about inner strength. Courage doesn't mean the absence of fear; instead, it's about acting despite fear. These encounters have a therapeutic impact, contributing significantly to the healing process. Positive affirmations reshape the inner dialogue, empowering individuals to counteract negative narratives born from heartbreak. Encouraged to create personal affirmations, readers find tools that align with their healing journeys.

Supportive friendships play a transformative role in fostering resilience. Through encouragement, friends serve as pillars of support, their words resonating in times of adversity. Anecdotes spotlight how friends uplift and validate each other, forging bonds that withstand the test of time. Shared experiences become a balm, with laughter and joy relieving emotional wounds. Whether engaging in fun activities or having honest conversations, these interactions underscore the importance of vulnerability in friendships.

Motivation derived from friendships spurs mutual growth, forming a collective support system where the success of one inspires others. Friendship, viewed as a partnership in healing, becomes an intrinsic force guiding individuals through their journeys. Cultivating such relationships offers solace, reinforcing the belief that together, resilience is achievable and inevitable.

In summation, this book weaves a narrative that mirrors the emotional highs and lows faced by young adults and those battling personal challenges. It is a testament to the resilience found amidst heartbreak, illuminating the path from self-discovery to independence. Readers will come away feeling seen, understood, and inspired, armed with the realization that they can navigate their unique journeys with courage and hope.

Finding a new sense of community becomes essential on this journey. The protagonist, Lucy, steps into volunteer work at the local animal shelter. Initially, she feels apprehensive and uncertain about connecting with new people after the heartbreak that weighed heavily on her. Yet, as she engages with the animals and the other volunteers, the warmth of shared purpose envelops her, making her realize that connections can form in unexpected places. The chatter of fellow volunteers fills her heart with a lightness she thought lost. Sophie, a friendly volunteer with an infectious laugh, quickly becomes a confidante, sharing her stories of heartbreak and recovery. Their conversations spark an understanding that, while their journeys are distinct, they are not alone in their struggles.

As Lucy spends more time at the shelter, she starts to find healing in caring for the animals, understanding that their need for love and companionship mirrors hers. One afternoon, she is particularly drawn to a shy stray dog named Max. His big brown eyes speak volumes of abandonment and fear, resonating with the echoes of her past. Lucy patiently begins to build trust with Max, discovering that as he learns to overcome his fears, so does she. Each small step forward, coaxing Max into the sunlight or teaching him simple commands, represents progress in her journey to embrace vulnerability again.

Weekends at the shelter become a ritual for Lucy. With Sophie by her side, they often joke and share stories, creating a space where laughter thrives amidst the chaos of life. Lucy experiences a renewed sense of belonging through these moments, appreciating how friendship can blossom while nurturing mutual growth. They talk about life, dreams, fears, and aspirations. One day, Sophie suggests organizing a community event at the shelter to foster more connections within the neighborhood. The idea excites Lucy, awakening her creativity and enthusiasm that she thought had faded.

Planning the event proves to be a refreshing distraction from her internal struggles. Lucy and Sophie brainstorm ideas, from pet adoption drives to interactive workshops on responsible pet care. The more they collaborate, the more Lucy's confidence flourishes. She communicates with local businesses, seeking donations and partnerships, and feels empowered to take charge of a project that could uplift others. This endeavor strengthens the bond between the two friends, reinforcing their commitment to support one another's growth.

On the day of the event, excitement electrifies the atmosphere. Lucy stands at the entrance, welcoming attendees with Sophie. The sound of laughter and joyful barking fills the air, creating an ambiance of hope and renewal. Lucy observes families, friends, and animal lovers coming together and feels immense pride in what they have made. As the day unfolds, she finds herself connected to her community in a way she hadn't anticipated, recognizing that healing often extends beyond personal experiences.

During a lull, Sophie nudges Lucy and says, "Look at all these people! You made this happen." For a moment, Lucy allows herself to cherish the compliment, smiling at Sophie before taking a deep breath. "I couldn't have done it without you," she replies, grateful for the shared journey. Their friendship provides a safety net, allowing Lucy to step outside her comfort zone, and in return, she encourages Sophie to confront her fears.

As the sun sets over the shelter, a sense of fulfillment washes over Lucy. She reflects on her journey, realizing that the embrace of community has filled the gaps left by heartbreak. Lucy now understands that the road to healing intertwines with the experiences of others, creating a rich tapestry of relationships. She feels lighter, recognizing how vulnerability and shared connections strengthen resilience rather than diminish it.

Weeks pass, and the shelter thrives, thanks to ongoing community support. Lucy finds her days filled with purpose, a stark contrast to the somber shadows that used to linger. Armed with hope, she continues to build bridges within her community while nurturing her bond with Max, who now runs freely, tail wagging and spirit soaring.

One breezy afternoon, Lucy sits outside with Sophie, sipping iced tea as they watch the sunset. Their conversation drifts from everyday topics to future aspirations. Sophie expresses her dreams of starting a nonprofit organization to support animal welfare. Lucy listens intently, feeling inspired by the fire in Sophie's eyes. As the thought forms in her mind, Lucy shares her aspiration to pursue art and channel her experiences into creating a mural for the shelter.

They dream together, envisioning a vibrant representation of their journey through heartbreak, resilience, and newfound joy. This collaborative goal strengthens their connection, reminding Lucy that creativity can be a powerful form of expression and healing.

Days turn into weeks, and planning for the mural takes shape. Lucy gathers supplies and sketches her ideas, pouring her emotions into every stroke. This project becomes a celebration of resilience, a tribute to new beginnings and the connections that lift her during tough times. Each brushstroke carries memories—the weight of heartbreak grows lighter, and the beauty of newfound strength shines through.

While painting at the shelter one evening, Sophie surprises Lucy with a little gathering of friends. They all bring food and drinks, transforming the work into a festive affair filled with laughter and camaraderie. Lucy feels overwhelmed by the support, valuing how these friendships contribute to her healing. In this space, vulnerability shifts from a burden to a source of connection and empowerment.

As they paint together, Lucy laughs, shares stories, and feels a sense of purpose she had thought lost in heartbreak. With each moment shared, she realizes that resilience is not merely a personal endeavor but a collective experience that reinforces the importance of community. As she takes a step back to admire their progress, she understands that true healing embraces solitude and connection. Both coexist beautifully in a world where every heartbeat resonates with shared stories, laughter, and hope.

CHAPTER 8

Healing Together

In the tapestry of teenage life, love often appears as both a thrilling adventure and an intricate puzzle. For young adults stepping into this world of emotions for the first time, the journey can feel overwhelming. Sometimes love feels like an exhilarating high, where everything seems possible because you're with someone who understands you. But alongside those highs come the lows—heartbreak that leaves you questioning everything you thought you knew about yourself and your relationships.

This book is about navigating the complicated terrain of love and heartbreak. It's for anyone who has ever felt the sting of unreturned affection, basked in the glow of mutual attraction, or fought to piece themselves together after something they were sure was real came undone. This isn't just a guide on how to deal with breakups or find love; it's an exploration of personal growth and healing, capturing the essence of what it means to be vulnerable, resilient, and ultimately human in our search for connection.

Imagine sitting down with a friend who knows exactly how you feel—a friend who listens and shares their stories of late-night talks and hidden fears. This is the essence of our story—finding healing through mutual support and understanding. Through open conversations about past wounds, we realize that being vulnerable with someone we trust can strengthen our bond. Sharing secrets may seem daunting at first, but it deepens intimacy and opens pathways of empathy, allowing us to truly see each other's struggles.

But healing isn't just about talking; it's about creating frameworks for support. Establishing boundaries while sharing creates a safe space where judgment is left at the door. We learn to listen actively, viewing honesty not as a weakness but as a cornerstone of our relationship. Together, we embark on journeys of symbolic healing, writing letters to our younger selves and engaging in acts that symbolize growth and understanding. These moments ground our pain and triumphs in reality, showing us the transformative power of shared experiences.

As we navigate this journey, we face the profound impact of forgiveness and reconciliation. Past grievances don't disappear overnight, but we create space for compassion by naming the hurt and acknowledging its presence. Communication becomes vital, bridging gaps in understanding as we express our feelings honestly. Through small acts of forgiveness, we redefine relationships built on respect and strength. New memories form the anchors of our healing journey, reminding us that love can endure trials and emerge stronger than before.

In piecing ourselves back together, there's a pivotal moment of reevaluation—a time to reflect on what truly matters. Individual aspirations and future dreams take center stage, helping clarify desires beyond love alone. Sharing these dreams ignites excitement and strengthens partnerships, encouraging us to pursue goals separately and together. As expectations shift and grow, we adjust gracefully, learning that flexibility is a testament to our resilience and adaptability.

Of course, none of this would be possible without empathy—the lifeline of any meaningful relationship. Engaging in active listening exercises teaches us the invaluable lesson of being present, not just hearing words but also understanding perspectives. By exploring each other's worlds, we dismantle misunderstandings and gain insight into each other's motivations and fears. Actual validation becomes habitual, fostering environments where we feel cared for and respected. A shared language of empathy evolves, transcending spoken words and rooting us deeply in love.

Love can be scary for some—letting someone in means risking parts of yourself. Yet here we discover that within vulnerability lies incredible strength. As we peel back layers of self-doubt and fear, we begin to appreciate the complexities of one another's paths to healing. Our shared journey teaches us that while we may travel solo at times, there is immense power in walking alongside someone who believes in you just as fiercely as you believe in them.

This is more than just a book about love; it's an invitation to explore what it means to heal and grow together, to forgive and forge new memories. It's a reminder that there's a pathway forward paved by empathy, understanding, and unwavering resilience amidst heartache and chaos. As you dive into this narrative, know it speaks directly to your experience and is designed to resonate with every challenge and aspiration you harbor. Let the stories within these pages remind you that you're never alone in your journey and that healing is always possible—especially when done together.

As we settle into these new dynamics, we explore how love manifests. It can be the sweet thrill of a first kiss, the warmth of a shared joke, or even the quiet support during tough times. James and Lily have been best friends since middle school, but lately, the air between them feels charged with something more. They spend hours discussing their dreams—the places they want to travel, the careers they aspire to, and the future they imagine. While reassuring each other of their friendship, there's an unspoken tension, a weight of possibility that neither dares to address outright.

Sitting under their favorite oak tree one afternoon, Lily turns to James, the sunlight filtering through the leaves casting playful shadows. "Do you ever think about us, like, really think about it?" she asks, her voice soft yet steady. James's heart races. He can hardly breathe but nods, unsure if he wants to jump into this conversation or pull back.

"All the time," he admits, his eyes locked onto hers. "But what if it ruins what we have?"

Their conversation explores what-ifs, fears, and dreams, ultimately revealing deeper emotions they've both kept under wraps. It becomes clear that love is not just about passion; it's intertwined with friendship, trust, and the desire to be indeed known. They leap, embracing their feelings instead of burying them under the pretense of normalcy.

Meanwhile, Sophia sits lost in thought. She's just come out of a rough breakup, reeling from the betrayal of someone she cherished. On the outside, she hides her hurt behind a smile, but inside, she feels shattered. One evening, she meets with her friends at the coffee shop where they always gather, clutching a warm latte. The chatter is light, focused on weekend plans, but Sophia can't help feeling detached. As their laughter fills the air, she finds it hard to relate.

Amid the noise, Emma, her closest friend, notices. "Soph, what's going on? You've been off lately," she remarks gently, concern in her voice. Sophia hesitates, torn between wanting to be honest and fearing the weight of her pain might bring everyone down. Eventually, the dam breaks, and she spills her heart. "I don't know how to get over him. It feels like every time I think about it, it just hurts more."

Emma reaches across the table, giving Sophia's hand a reassuring squeeze. "It's okay to feel that way. Healing takes time," she assures her. They delve into the conversation, sharing their experiences with love and loss. They create a safe space where vulnerability feels accepted, and slowly, Sophia begins to articulate her struggles.

Sharing stories becomes a common thread in their group, weaving together experiences that remind them they are not alone in their journeys. They learn that even in heartbreak, laughter can seep through the cracks, offering a glimmer of hope. More than support, this becomes a healing ritual—sharing music, exchanging books, and exploring new hobbies together. Each laugh and tear adds to their understanding, reinforcing the idea that love exists in many forms.

As the weeks go by, Sophia starts redefining herself beyond her heartbreak. She immerses herself in painting, expressing emotions she couldn't articulate before. On tough days, she creates vivid images of sunsets and serene landscapes, pouring her feelings onto the canvas. Her friends encourage her to showcase her art at a local exhibit, a leap she finds terrifying yet exhilarating. Sharing her vulnerability through art transforms her pain into a powerful narrative of hope and resilience.

At the exhibit, as she stands by her pieces, she witnesses strangers connecting with her work, sparking conversations about love, loss, and recovery. It becomes evident that the stories we tell don't live in isolation; they resonate deeply with others, forging unexpected connections. After one such conversation, a girl approaches Sophia, eyes misty. "Your painting reminded me of my journey. I lost someone I loved too," she says, gratitude lingering.

Sophia takes a deep breath, feeling her heart swell. These moments illuminate why sharing becomes vital—through shared experiences, healing finds community. It chisels away at the feeling of isolation, showing that we can grow together. As she leaves the exhibit, she feels lighter, aware that while the past still holds weight, it no longer defines her.

Amidst these transformations, friendships deepen as love becomes an overarching theme. The conversations surrounding fears morph into discussions about dreams again—what's next, who they want to become, and how they want their lives to unfold. James's newfound relationship with Lily makes him more open, and he finds joy in exploring emotions without fearing losing their friendship.

As they walk home one night, hands brushing, he asks her, "What do you want for us moving forward? What do you envision?" Lily pauses, staring up at the stars, contemplating the trajectory of their relationship. "I want honesty," she replies. "I don't want versions of the truth that hold back what we feel. If we're going to do this, let's be all in."

James smiles, his heart swelling. The clarity of her words cracks open the door to deeper intimacy. In this moment, they pledge to embrace every facet of their love, no matter how challenging.

Their collective journeys remind everyone that love and healing are ongoing processes. They learn from one another, proving that the bravest thing one can do is to be accurate, recognizing that each step forward is not just about love but also about learning to love oneself in the midst of it all. As the chapters of their lives unfold, they step into the future equipped with empathy, courage, and the unwavering belief that tomorrow holds new possibilities.

CHAPTER 9

Embracing Change

In the journey of life, change is inevitable. The relentless tide shapes our experiences, carving out the tapestry of who we are and who we have yet to become. This truth can be daunting and exhilarating for young hearts navigating the tumultuous landscape of love for the first time. We dive into relationships drawn by the allure of connection, and along the way, we encounter unexpected challenges that test the very core of our beings.

I remember my first experience with love—it was a whirlwind filled with moments of pure joy and others of heart-wrenching sadness. In those tender years, when emotions feel so raw, and everything seems magnified, understanding that change is a constant companion in our lives can sometimes slip past us. Yet, within these shifting sands, we find the seeds of growth. Embracing change allows us to evolve, adapt to new realities, and discover aspects of ourselves we never knew existed.

At the heart of this evolution is acceptance. Resisting change often leads to stagnation and heartache, while acceptance opens doors to previously unimagined possibilities. Imagine a world where love doesn't challenge your beliefs or push you beyond your comfort zone. Would you truly grow if everything stayed the same? Through love, we learn not only about others but also about ourselves. These experiences force us to confront our fears and step bravely into the unknown, leading to deeper connections and healthier dynamics in our relationships.

Yet, amidst personal transformation, societal expectations loom large. They dictate how we should behave, whom we should love, and our relationships. As we navigate these pressures, we uncover the strength to remain true to ourselves. Balancing societal norms with personal desires requires courage and authenticity. I've had moments in my own life when stepping against the tide felt like small acts of rebellion—necessary steps toward self-acceptance.

Love, with all its uncertainties and unpredictabilities, invites us to embrace the unknown. This isn't always easy, especially when the future appears hazy, but taking leaps of faith can lead to unexpected joy and fulfillment. We've all heard stories or lived them ourselves of the transformative power of choosing love despite uncertainty. The daring to hope and trust becomes a testament to resilience.

Through our interactions with others, we begin to see the world through different lenses. Whether it's sitting across from someone sharing their story or finding common ground in a disagreement, these exchanges enrich our perspectives. Every relationship offers the potential for profound insight, teaching us empathy and deepening our understanding. I treasure the conversations where contrasting viewpoints bring clarity and fortify bonds with those I love.

Moreover, challenges, though difficult now, are ripe with growth opportunities. I've often reflected on past adversities only to realize they were the catalysts for some of the most meaningful changes in my life. Gratitude for these experiences becomes a powerful tool, turning setbacks into celebrations and paving the way for more substantial connections with those we hold dear. By embracing these shifts in perspective, we nurture our relationships and ourselves.

In every partnership, acknowledging milestones is an essential practice—markers of evolution that honor individuality and shared journeys. Celebrating victories, whether quiet achievements or monumental successes, reinforces the commitment built over time. Each milestone represents a linear path forward and a dynamic interplay between two people growing together and separately.

Maintaining a balance between individuality and partnership is a delicate dance. It calls for keen awareness of one's desires and boundaries. Personal growth fuels the health of any relationship, ensuring that we don't lose sight of who we are even as we integrate into another's life. Nurturing individual pursuits rejuvenates the partnership, keeping it vibrant and authentic. The ability to cherish mutual interests while valuing time apart strengthens bonds, allowing space for personal exploration and shared dreams alike.

Encouragement plays a significant role here. Love can inspire each partner's aspirations, acting as a catalyst for achieving personal and relational goals. When we empower each other's growth, we create environments rich in support and respect—a fertile ground where love can thrive.

Reflecting on past relationships offers invaluable lessons that shape our present and future. Our histories are filled with moments of both pain and joy, each contributing to the tapestry of wisdom we carry forward. Pain, in particular, can transform into profound insights, guiding us toward healthier engagements. Forgiveness becomes a critical element of this healing process, liberating us from the burdens of yesterday. Letting go makes room for new beginnings, informed by the resilience we've cultivated through previous experiences.

This book is an invitation to explore these themes through relatable narratives. It speaks to those who seek understanding on their path to loving and being loved. As we embark on this journey together, may you find comfort in knowing that change is not something to fear but rather to embrace. With each chapter, you will uncover ways to celebrate newfound perspectives, navigate the delicate balance between self and togetherness, and build resilience from the lessons learned along the way.

Ultimately, this celebration of love's transformative power encourages you to reflect on your experiences and prepare for the beautiful unpredictability of what lies ahead. Let's embrace change hand in hand, allowing it to guide us toward deeper insights and connections, enriching our lives with every step. When I think about my experiences with love, I can't help but recall the friendships that blossomed alongside these romantic entanglements. They taught me just as much, if not more, about connection and change. Close friends often become our first teachers in the realm of emotions. They hold mirrors to our souls, revealing truths we may not want to see but desperately need to. I remember sharing late-night conversations filled with laughter and tears—moments where vulnerability made us feel closer, every word weaving a thread into the fabric of our bond.

One friend, in particular, stands out. Mia and I met in high school, two shy girls who bonded over our love for poetry. We scribbled verses in notebooks, sharing our dreams and fears. As we faced heartbreaks and triumphs, our relationship deepened. I learned from her how to voice my emotions and express my thoughts without fear of judgment. Our late-night talks transformed into heart-to-heart sessions, where we would dissect our love lives, relishing the chaos and confusion together. Each experience was an opportunity to grow, and our friendship served as a safe space for the mess that often accompanied young love.

As we ventured into different relationships, the lessons from our friendship echoed in those connections. I started to recognize the patterns—the moments when I became afraid to express my feelings out of concern for what others would think. Every time I held back, I felt a little piece of myself slip away. But in the warmth of Mia's understanding, I realized that love should encourage openness, not stifle it. Our conversations made me consider the importance of being true to myself in romantic situations, reminding me that honesty creates a foundation for lasting connections.

Some friendships require more effort as outside influences tug at their seams. As Mia and I grew closer, I noticed the shift that sometimes happens when life demands more of our attention and energy. Our paths began to diverge; she focused on her studies while I immersed myself in a relationship that consumed my time. The guilt of neglecting our friendship lingered, especially as I watched her withdraw a bit. I learned that love in any form demands balance; both romantic relationships and friendships thrive when the investment is mutual.

This realization became a vital lesson in self-awareness. I went through conversations with her where I had to explain my feelings and navigate the art of reassurance. “Mia, you’re my best friend, and I don’t want to lose you,” I told her one evening. “I need you to understand that my love life doesn’t change my feelings for you.” She smiled and nodded in response, assuring me that our friendship would weather the storms. Those discussions became crucial in redefining our relationship, emphasizing that love, in all forms, is about maintaining connections even as life evolves.

We learned to schedule our time—fun coffee dates transformed into cherished rituals, bringing us back together amidst our chaotic lives. These moments intensified our understanding of one another and reminded us of our support. The way we uplifted each other served as a foundation for our romantic endeavors. By nurturing our friendship, we cultivated a sense of security, reinforcing that love flourishes when watered with effort and attention.

As things developed, I couldn’t ignore the lessons arising from unforeseen challenges. Some friendships may not withstand the test of time, especially when they face external pressures or misunderstandings. I witnessed this distinctly when another friend, Sarah, entered a love affair with someone who didn’t share our values. The way she changed and our friend group shifted around her was eye-opening. I observed how love could sometimes pull individuals in different directions, causing rifts that felt insurmountable. It made me realize that, sometimes, love could lead to painful separations as personal beliefs clashed louder than affection.

Yet, it also highlighted the importance of support. Instead of withdrawing from Sarah, I tried to remain part of her journey, letting her know she wasn't alone. We had intense conversations filled with frustration and fear as I expressed concerns about her relationship, emphasizing the importance of discerning love that uplifts instead of holds back. "I care about you, but you deserve someone who aligns with your heart," I reminded her, hoping to guide her toward clarity. Watching her struggle felt similar to watching a storm cloud blur a sunny day. I wanted her to find her way back to clear skies.

Through these experiences, I realized that love isn't restricted to one type or person. It encompasses many facets, each teaching us something unique about ourselves and those we care about. Each relationship, whether friendship or romance, is an opportunity to learn and evolve. They nurture our capacity for empathy, force us to confront harsh truths, and ultimately encourage us to embrace that ever-present change.

These themes of love and friendship didn't just reside within my experiences; they were echoed in the stories shared by others. Friends often highlighted the lessons learned—some the result of joy, others from heartache, each adding layers to the understanding fabric. I listened intently as insights flowed like a river, merging to create a swirling wisdom current. The richness in these exchanges became fuel; they motivated me to continue exploring the depths of love, friendships, and the growth that comes from them.

In this exploration, I came to appreciate the beauty of shared experiences, the emotional tapestry woven from various threads of our lives. Each person we connect with adds nuance to our narrative. I felt grateful for the struggles, for they underscored the necessary work involved in fostering relationships. We don't always realize the strength we develop through love until we look back and see how far we have come.

This continued journey toward understanding reminds us that change, while daunting, is a vital underpinning to all relationships. The paths we walk may twist and turn, but we keep moving forward, hand in hand with others who share our journey. What awaits us is a canvas yet to come alive with the colors of our experiences. Each moment spent embracing this truth brings us closer to a fulfilling understanding of love and the connections we cherish.

CHAPTER 10

A Love Reimagined

As we end this journey, there's a sense of fullness, a richness that reflects not just the characters' evolution but our understanding of love and life. The narrative has shown us that love, at its core, is about growth — as individuals and together.

Imagine love as a garden. It flourishes with time, patience, nurturing, and sometimes change. Our protagonists learned that personal dreams are essential seeds in this garden. They chose to water those seeds, pursuing individual goals while sharing their hopes. Through this, they discovered an important truth: fulfillment outside the relationship enhances the one within it. By supporting each other's passions and challenges, they built a supportive environment where love could thrive.

Communication played a pivotal role throughout their journey. Evident, open-hearted dialogue became the lighthouse that guided them through uncertainty. Being vulnerable about aspirations wasn't easy, yet it strengthened their connection. They learned to share fears and dreams honestly, making tough conversations safe rather than scary. It was in these moments of transparency that trust was cultivated, ensuring resilience against future waves.

A significant chapter unfolded when they recognized the need for boundaries. This wasn't about distance but respect. Giving each other space fostered independence while ensuring emotional intimacy. Their relationship thrived on individuality, understanding that true closeness comes from two whole people, not halves trying to make a complete.

Respecting limits allowed them to keep the dance of love graceful and genuine.

They also discovered joy in celebrating milestones, be they small or grand. Acknowledging personal and shared achievements infused their story with vibrancy and unity. These celebrations reminded them — and us — of how far they've come and the significance of every step taken together. As readers, we take away the importance of honoring victories along our paths and finding power in reflection and gratitude.

These experiences teach a valuable lesson about integrating past learnings into daily life. Self-care emerged as a crucial pillar for maintaining their healthy relationship. Prioritizing mental health translated into more affluent, meaningful connections, showcasing self-love's transformative power. Practicing routine self-care brought harmony, reinforcing that well-being creates a sturdy foundation for love to build upon.

Creating rituals added another layer of intimacy. Simple traditions carved out intentional spaces for connection and joy, highlighting that magic often lies in the mundane. The couple found laughter and closeness through shared activities, proving that lasting relationships are nurtured in everyday tenderness.

Navigating conflicts with empathy and respect became another cornerstone of their story. They embraced healthy communication strategies, turning disagreements into opportunities for growth. Disputes no longer threatened their bond; respectful dialogue deepened their understanding of each other. Their commitment to a growth mindset allowed curiosity to replace defensiveness, transforming challenges into pathways for more vital unity.

Moreover, leaning on a support network fortified their relationship. Friends and family provided balance and perspective, reminding them — and us — of love's expansive reach beyond romantic ties. Valuing input from trusted companions enhanced their growth, creating a robust web of care surrounding their journey.

As we look toward the horizon, there's a hopeful outlook painted across their future. Envisioning dreams together fueled motivation, weaving personal ambitions into their shared story. This collective dreaming aligned their paths, fostering teamwork and a shared vision. Hope became a guiding light amidst uncertainties, illuminating possibilities even in shadowy moments.

Accepting life's unpredictability prepared them for what lay ahead. Acknowledging potential obstacles grounded their expectations in reality while embracing imperfection freed them to live spontaneously. Their story teaches us the power of flexibility in navigating life's turns, encouraging us to dance with life rather than resist its rhythm.

Positivity became the final brushstroke in their future portrait. Adopting an affirming mindset and surrounding themselves with uplifting company fortified their resolve against adversity. Positivity wasn't a denial of hardships but a choice to see beyond them, strengthening their bond by cultivating love's brightest colors.

As they pledged continuous growth — as individuals and partners — they cemented their dedication to lifelong learning. Their understanding that love is an ever-evolving journey reminds us that progress is a shared achievement, deepening bonds through the tapestry of changing seasons.

Reflecting on their transformation underscores the book's lasting impact. The journey taught them authenticity, emphasizing the strength of being true to oneself and others. Vulnerability showcased its power, fostering deeper emotional connections and guiding choices with an honest heart.

They embraced love's complexity, savoring its joys and pains as integral parts of their experience. Understanding love as multifaceted allowed them to appreciate its depth, enriching their interactions with compassion and patience.

Cherished memories became cornerstones of future growth. Reflecting on shared experiences highlighted their commitment, infusing their legacy with stories of resilience and healing. The journey inspired transformations within themselves and those around them, igniting conversations about love's transformative nature.

Their relationship stands as a testament to love's enduring power. It's a legacy of healing that extends beyond their narrative, touching lives and sparking change in unexpected places. Pledging to continue sharing their story radiates positivity outward, inviting others to explore their journeys of love and self-discovery.

In closing, may we carry forward the lessons of love's complexities and the beauty of its growth. Let us value both struggles and celebrations encountered along the way, knowing that every moment contributes to the masterpiece of our own stories. As you turn the final page, may your heart stay open to love's endless possibilities, nurturing your garden with hope, purpose, and authenticity.

Their journey continued as they delved deeper into the essence of companionship. They began to see that love wasn't solely defined by romantic moments but by acts of kindness and understanding. Simple gestures, like a warm cup of coffee waiting on the table or a thoughtful text during a long day, became the threads that wove their lives together even more tightly. These acts represented the small but significant ways they honored one another, proving that love could be expressed in many ways. They understood that nurturing love could be as straightforward as listening attentively when the other spoke, validating their feelings, and genuinely showing interest in one another's day.

They also embraced spontaneity as a vital ingredient in their love story. It was common for them to find themselves on unexpected adventures, whether that meant an impromptu road trip or a late-night exploration of their city's hidden gems. Each adventure served as a reminder that love thrived in instability and the unpredictable moments they carved out together. They learned to let go of rigid schedules and plans, allowing joy to take the lead instead. This freedom to explore and play became a cherished aspect of their relationship, adding layers of pleasure and excitement that enriched their bond.

Moreover, they recognized the importance of gratitude as an everyday practice. Each evening, they set aside time to share what they appreciated about each other. It didn't have to be grand; the little things often sparked the most warmth. "I loved how you smiled at me today" or "Thanks for your support during my meeting," highlighted their acknowledgment of each other's efforts and strengths. Expressing gratitude created an emotional reservoir that fortified their love, helping them navigate more challenging times with resilience. It was a gentle reminder of the goodness in their relationship, reinforcing their commitment to see the best in one another, even when challenges arose.

As they navigated career changes and personal growth, they faced seasons of uncertainty. Support took on new meanings during these times. They committed to showing up fully for each other, whether lending an ear or offering insights based on their diverse experiences. "I know it's tough right now, but I'm here," was a phrase often exchanged between them. This assurance fostered trust, illustrating that love wasn't always about having answers but cultivating a safe space to explore fears and aspirations together. They learned that standing by one another through uncertainties brought them closer and allowed deeper conversations about their future and dreams.

They also welcomed the concept of forgiveness as a necessary element in love's growth. Misunderstandings and mistakes emerged, as they naturally would in any relationship. Instead of allowing resentment to fester, they approached their conflicts with open hearts and minds. They knew that holding onto past grievances would only hinder their progress. "Let's take a moment to talk about this" became a mantra that eased tension. This approach allowed them to address issues head-on, fostering a healthy exchange of thoughts and feelings, leading to mutual understanding and healing. They cleared emotional debris through forgiveness, reaffirming their commitment to one another and paving paths toward deeper connections.

Interactions with their extended families also played a crucial role in their evolving relationship. They began to appreciate how each family brought unique dynamics and histories. Meeting relatives fostered understanding and acceptance of one another's backgrounds. They learned to navigate differing traditions and values gracefully, knowing this diversity only enriched their relationship. Family gatherings showcased the blending of their worlds, illustrating that love was about inclusion and integrating everyone into their narrative. They supported each other through family experiences, from celebrations to challenges, reinforcing that love expanded beyond romance and embraced a larger circle of care and connection.

In this journey of love, they also realized the impact of the community around them. Friendships became essential support systems that nourished their relationship. Sharing experiences with close friends led to discussions about love, self-discovery, and the essentials of healthy partnerships. "What works for you?" and "How do you handle disagreements?" became common inquiries as they sought insights from their peer network. These conversations emphasized that love wasn't only confined to romantic partnerships; it thrived in friendships, too. They learned to celebrate their friends' achievements, offering encouragement and camaraderie, strengthening their bond and sense of belonging.

As the seasons changed, they often contemplated the beauty of what lay ahead. Together, they painted visions of their future—of travels they wished to embark upon, dreams they longed to chase, and the life they hoped to build. These conversations, filled with laughter and enthusiasm, illustrated their shared commitment to growth. "Can you imagine us exploring ancient ruins in another country?" sparked a dialogue that led to tangible plans that grounded their dreams in reality. They reinforced that building a future required teamwork, aligning their aspirations to cultivate a shared journey.

Their willingness to face challenges head-on and embrace change fortified their foundation. Every upheaval acted as a reminder of their resilience. They held each other tightly during turbulent times, knowing that as long as they had each other, they could overcome any storm. During these moments, I encouraged them to trust in their adaptability as a couple, allowing for organic growth as they shaped their lives together. They envisioned that love was not a linear path but an ever-evolving dance filled with unexpected turns, graceful moves, and sometimes the occasional misstep.

As they continued forward, they focused on their journey and how they could contribute meaningfully to the world around them. Engaging in community service became an avenue through which they could share their love externally. Whether volunteering at local shelters or participating in community clean-ups, they discovered the joy of giving back together. This shared purpose strengthened their connection, reminding them of love's expansive power that rippled beyond just their relationship. They sought opportunities to uplift others through their actions, understanding that thriving in love meant lifting those around them.

With each passing day, their garden of love blossomed in ways they never imagined. Like any living thing, they knew nurturing required constant effort. They embraced love's challenges as growth opportunities rather than obstacles. This ever-evolving narrative showcased the power of patience, empathy, and commitment to maintaining harmony in their relationship while continually enhancing their understanding of each other and the world around them.

Conclusion

Reflecting on the past can be a powerful catalyst for growth. As I take a moment to look back at the rollercoaster journey of emotions that unfolded throughout this story, I see how every twist and turn played a crucial role in shaping the protagonist's understanding of love. Much like our experiences with first loves, the highs were breathtaking, filled with moments of connection and joy that seemed almost magical. Yet, during the more challenging times—the uncertainties, misunderstandings, and heartaches—the depth of her journey came to light.

She learned that love is not always straightforward through these ups and downs. It often presents itself in ways we least expect, pushing us to question what we believe about ourselves and others. However, within these trials lies the opportunity for profound personal growth. Each turbulent chapter in this narrative mirrored the complexities of first love that many of us experience. It showcased the beauty of falling for someone and the strength required to push through adversity when things do not go according to plan.

Throughout the story, the protagonist discovers resilience; she finds the courage to embrace vulnerability, realizing that opening up her heart, even when there is a risk of pain, is vital to forming authentic connections. She learned that love is not merely defined by joy but is woven into the fabric of life's storms—it is about weathering them with someone who stands beside you, hand in hand. Even amidst challenges, her ability to redefine what love meant demonstrated an evolving perspective—a testament to her growth and newfound maturity.

Equally important was her awareness of societal norms and expectations pressing down upon her. We have all felt those pressures at times. Perhaps it was the judgmental whispers from peers or the weight of conventional standards dictating how relationships should unfold. These external voices could have easily swayed her decisions, leading her away from what mattered. Yet, standing firm in her beliefs and desires showed incredible strength. Her journey reiterates the significance of following one's heart, even when the world seems to be telling you otherwise. Happiness should never be compromised, nor should it conform to others' definitions—it is a profoundly personal journey.

This tale resonates with a universal truth: the intricacies of love are tied to our evolution. And though the path may feel daunting at times, holding onto hope and faith can lead to unexpected beauty in life's tapestry. As we step forward, like our protagonist, let us carry the lessons etched in our hearts. Love, no matter its form, holds immense power. It can heal, inspire, and create new possibilities, even when born from sacrifices or heartbreaks.

We find ourselves at a juncture where love does not conform to a single definition. Instead, it ebbs and flows, teaching us valuable lessons about ourselves and the dynamics with those around us. By embracing everything we have learned, whether cherished memories or painful reminders, we pave the way toward future clarity and compassion in our relationships.

As young adults grappling with our place in the world, let us embrace these transformative journeys. They mold us, enrich our understanding of empathy, and cultivate the wisdom essential for thriving in love and life alike. The beauty of storytelling, after all, is its ability to mirror the essence of reality while providing insights into matters close to our hearts.

And so, as you close this chapter, remember that it is simply one part of an ever-evolving journey. Harness hope as your guiding light, trusting its capacity to lead you toward meaningful connections and renewed perspectives. Allow these stories to encourage introspection and resilience—qualities essential for navigating whatever lies ahead.

In conclusion, thank you for joining us on this poignant exploration of love and self-discovery. Know that within each heartbeat lies potential—for healing, inspiration, and creating unfathomable possibilities. You, too, hold the power needed to carve out paths uncharted yet brimming with promise, should you dare to seize them.

With hearts wide open, let us cherish love's multifaceted nature—a force capable of transforming lives unexpectedly and teaching us invaluable truths along life's winding road. Here's to embarking on our unique journeys equipped with newfound wisdom, strengthened resolve, and inspired vision drawn from shared narratives echoing timelessly across generations.

Part 2

Overcoming Obstacles on the Road to Romance

Journey Through Love's Challenges

Contents

Chapter 11: Navigating Personal Insecurities

Chapter 12: Breaking Through Societal Pressures

Chapter 13: Embracing Vulnerability

Chapter 14: Communicating with Clarity

Chapter 15: Fostering Emotional Resilience

Chapter 16: Building Mutual Respect

Chapter 17: Growing Together in Love

Chapter 18: Balancing Independence and Togetherness

Chapter 19: Finding Strength in Adversity

Chapter 20: Realizing the Transformative Power of Love

Chapter 11

Navigating Personal Insecurities

What if your greatest fears and insecurities aren't just roadblocks to romance but stepping stones to something deeper and more meaningful? Imagine a world where each obstacle you face in love is a chance to grow and forge connections that are not only profound but also transformative. Welcome to "Overcoming Obstacles on the Road to Romance," a heartfelt exploration of the journey toward authentic love.

For many young adults, the quest for genuine connection can feel overwhelming. The pressure to meet societal expectations and the weight of personal insecurities often complicate this pursuit. Yet within these challenges lies an opportunity to learn, evolve, and discover what truly matters in relationships. Our book is dedicated to illuminating these experiences, offering relatable narratives reflecting youthful romance's intricate dance.

In today's world, the path to love is rarely straightforward. Our primary audience, young adults aged 16-24, often navigate a labyrinth of emotions and external pressures. Questions like "How can I overcome my insecurities in relationships?" or "What are common societal pressures that affect young love?" are prevalent. Yet, they rarely receive the thoughtful exploration they deserve. This book aims to clarify, offering insights and strategies to empower readers on their romantic journeys.

You'll meet characters who mirror your own experiences, individuals grappling with similar challenges, and who ultimately uncover the resilience needed to create meaningful connections. This isn't just a collection of stories—it's a guide woven together by the theme of resilience, illustrating how overcoming obstacles can lead to growth and understanding in love.

The journey through this book promises transformation. Love has the power to heal and empower, turning adversity into an opportunity for growth and deeper connection. You'll witness how characters navigate personal insecurities, societal influences, and the myriad pressures of being young and in love. Their stories serve as a mirror and a lantern, reflecting your experiences while lighting the way forward.

As we delve into these narratives, we'll explore common insecurities that plague many young adults. Whether it's social comparison, body image issues, or the fear of rejection, we understand that these feelings often create barriers to forming meaningful relationships. Recognizing and addressing these insecurities can foster healthier dynamics, encouraging open communication and deeper connections.

Self-esteem plays a crucial role in navigating love. It directly influences relationship satisfaction and the ability to set boundaries. Readers will see the importance of nurturing self-worth through our characters and understand how a healthy self-image allows for greater confidence in relationships. This confidence, in turn, encourages authenticity and fosters more robust interactions with partners.

Building self-confidence is a journey that we embark on together. Through practical techniques like affirmations, setting achievable goals, and engaging in new activities, the book offers tools to help you cultivate self-assurance in both personal and romantic contexts. Each page is designed to inspire courage, inviting you to step outside your comfort zone and embrace new experiences that enrich your life.

And as we traverse these pages, the ultimate goal becomes clear: learning to love and accept oneself. Self-love is the cornerstone of healthy relationships and personal happiness. Embracing who you are, with all your imperfections, allows for genuine connections with others. This book emphasizes the significance of this acceptance, guiding you toward a place of inner peace and fulfillment.

Reading "Overcoming Obstacles on the Road to Romance" is about more than finding answers. It's about connecting with stories that resonate, finding solace in shared struggles, and collecting insights that inspire growth. For those who enjoy young adult fiction that combines romance with personal development themes, this journey will captivate your imagination and touch your heart.

Life's challenges are inevitable, but love offers a powerful counterbalance—a force that transforms and sustains us through adversity. As you navigate your path, remember that every hurdle is a lesson, leading you closer to the connection that can profoundly change your life. Here, you'll find the encouragement to embrace your romantic journey despite the hurdles that may arise.

This book is for anyone seeking to deepen their understanding of love and relationships. It's for the dreamers, the hopeful romantics, and the resilient souls who believe in the transformative power of love. As you engage with these stories, let them inspire you to forge stronger bonds, nurture your self-worth, and discover the depths of resilience within you.

In a world that often feels chaotic and overwhelming, your journey toward authentic love may seem daunting—yet, within these challenging moments, we indeed come alive. So join us as we embark on this heartfelt exploration, where every obstacle is an opportunity to grow, and every challenge is a chance to connect more deeply with ourselves and those we love.

Chapter 12

Breaking Through Societal Pressures

In a world brimming with swirling expectations and vibrant possibilities, young adults stand on the edge of defining their unique stories in love and relationships. Yet, amid this exhilarating journey, an invisible web of societal norms often attempts to dictate the paths they might traverse. These norms, woven into the very fabric of our culture, whisper subtle suggestions about who to love, how to express it, and when it ought to unfold. In this book, we embark on a quest to unravel these threads—inviting you to explore them and reclaim your narrative critically.

For those navigating the spheres of love in their late teens and early twenties, the struggle between external pressures and personal authenticity is indisputable. Traditional dating customs can feel like echoes from another era, shaping decisions based on criteria that may not be. It's crucial to pause and question whether conforming to such scripts genuinely seethe'sserheart's heart's true desires. Examining these influences opens doors to discovering what truly matters to each individual.

The digital landscape adds another layer of complexity, where social media often paints illusions of perfect romances. These online portrayals, while captivating, can lead to unhealthy comparisons and unrealistic expectations. The curated moments shared on screens rarely capture auconnections'ections' messy, beautiful reality. Understanding this distinction empowers you to foster healthier perceptions of love—ones grounded in truth rather than carefully selected snapshots.

Cultural differences further enrich the tapestry of relationship expectations, encouraging introspection on how diverse backgrounds shape romantic ideals. Whether emone'sng one's cultural heritage or blending different traditions, this awareness enables a profound understanding of love's multifaceted expressions. It invites an openness that celebrates varying perspectives, nurturing relationships that are not only compassionate but deeply enriched by diversity.

Amidst all this, the call to embrace individuality rings clear. In a society that sometimes demands conformity, staying true to oneself becomes an act of courage. Recognizing and honoring your values—and choosing partners aligned with them—creates space for genuine connections to flourish. When you decline to adhere strictly to societal molds, you gift yourself the freedom to love your love's journey on your terms.

Peer pressure adds yet another dimension to this exploration. Friends and acquaintances, knowingly or unknowingly, can sway decisions through direct suggestions or subtle cues. Navigating these dynamics with awareness allows for more conscious choices. By recognizing peer influences, you equip yourself with resilience, learning to assert what genuinely feels right for you.

Empowering yourself in dating involves mastering strategies that support declaring your preferences. Open communication and setting boundaries reinforce self-advocacy. This empowerment stems from a foundation of confidence and authenticity, reminding us all that compatibility is not just about mutual attraction but also alignione'sth one's deepest desires.

Within the gentle yet transformative realm of self-reflection, clarity emerges. Taking time to delve into your motivations and aspirations illuminates paths that align with true intentions—such intentionality fosters relationships where harmony prevails—a dance between inner truths and external experiences. Encouragingly, surrounding oneself with supportive friendships creates a buffer against negative influences, reinforcing that you are never alone in this journey.

And so, maintaining authenticity within relationships becomes paramount. Vulnerability, though daunting, can forge deeper connections beyond the surfacesurfaceIt'sel. It's about sharing who we are, our insecurities, and all with others who respect and accept us as we are. This acceptance lays the groundwork for compassion-nurturing bonds where love embraces imperfections.

Knowing when to compromise while standing firm is equally essential. Healthy compromises enhance relationships without eroding individual authenticity. It requires thoughtful evaluation of personal values and a willingness to balance interactions that reflect shared growth. Celebrating individuality strengthens unity within partnerships, promoting respect for differences and cultivating an environment where both partners thrive.

Fear often lurks in the shadows of judgment or rejection. Yet confronting these fears brings honesty and openness into relationships. Realizing true love encompasses flaws fosters security, inviting vulnerability where acceptance flourishes. A compassionate environment reduces fears, allowing genuine exchanges to unfold naturally.

Balancing personal desires with societal expectations becomes a graceful dance. Identifying what truly matters encourages you to articulate dreams and goals clearly. Writing down aspirations provides focus and guiding choices that resonate deeply with inner truths. While family expectations may weigh heavily, open conversations help mitigate pressures without losing individuality. Understanding that disagreeing with familial values can be part of personal growth encourages forging paths true to oneself.

Ultimately, crafting a love story that reflects your essence is the most fulfilling journey. Navigating the crossroads of societal influences and personal aspirations reveals narratives uniquely yours. Celebrating these distinct journeys conveys that authenticity breeds lasting connections— a love's power to transform, nurture, and uplift.

This book is your companion in exploring love amid the surrounding influences. As you turn its pages, embrace the opportunity to define your path—one imbued with emotional depth, resilience, and transformative magic. oHere's. Here's to unraveling the tapestry of societal expectations and weaving your own extraordinary story of romance and self-discovery.

Chapter 13
Embracing Vulnerability

In the tapestry of human experience, few threads are as deeply interwoven into the fabric of our lives as love and relationships. For young adults standing on the precipice of adulthood, navigating this complex terrain can be as exhilarating as daunting. At an age where emotions run deep, and connections shape our understanding of the world, the quest for authentic love becomes both a challenge and an adventure. Welcome to a journey through the nuances of vulnerability—a path that leads to deeper emotional intimacy and transformative self-discovery.

At its core, vulnerability is more than just letting someone in; it's about showing up as our most authentic selves and daring to share our dreams, fears, and desires. It invites us to drop the masks and armor we've constructed over time and embrace the raw, unfiltered essence of who we are. This openness, though scary at times, has the potential to forge connections so profound that they redefine what it means to know and be known by another person honestly.

Yet despite its undeniable power, vulnerability often gets a bad rap. Many of us grow up equating it with weakness, taught to guard our hearts and shield ourselves from emotional exposure. But what if, instead, we saw vulnerability as strength? What if being honest about our feelings wasn't something to be feared but celebrated? By embracing this mindset, we open the door to relationships built on trust and mutual respect, where authenticity reigns supreme.

Throughout history, countless love stories have demonstrated the unparalleled strength that arises from vulnerability. Take the couple who, amidst the chaos of life, decided to share their insecurities and found solace in doing so. Their shared vulnerability became the balm that soothed their fears, allowing them to face challenges together and emerge stronger. Or consider the pair who learned that expressing their needs and concerns honestly prevented misunderstandings and cultivated a culture of open dialogue. These narratives illuminate the transformative power of vulnerability, serving as beacons of hope and inspiration.

But embracing vulnerability isn't always easy. The fear of emotional exposure is a formidable barrier that many grapple with. The voice whispers caution, urging us to stay concealed and safe. Yet, ironically, it's through confronting these fears that we find liberation. By recognizing the patterns of avoidance that hold us back and reframing vulnerability as an opportunity for growth, we dismantle the walls that hinder genuine connection.

Contrary to popular belief, emotional exposure is not a reckless leap into the unknown. Instead, it's a calculated step towards authenticity—exploring oneself and one's relationship with others. By perceiving vulnerability as a pathway to meaningful connections, we cultivate a mindset that celebrates emotional risks. We learn that each act of openness, no matter how small, marks progress toward more prosperous relationships. Sharing personal anecdotes and celebrating these moments of courage encourage us to venture further down this path.

Integral to embracing vulnerability is establishing honest communication, the foundation of trust. In relationships, honesty isn't merely about truthfulness—it's about creating an environment where both partners feel secure in voicing thoughts and emotions without fearing judgment. Active listening plays a pivotal role here, fostering a sense of being heard and valued. When we fully engage with our partner's words, we create a space where deeper emotions can surface and be understood.

Furthermore, expressing our needs openly is vital. Addressing concerns early prevents simmering issues from boiling over later, ensuring trust remains intact. When integrated into every facet of a relationship, communication acts like regular maintenance, keeping the lines of connection solid and resilient.

Creating a safe space where vulnerability can thrive requires intention and effort. It's about building an emotional sanctuary where judgments are left at the door, and empathy takes center stage. Such environments allow partners to be themselves, sharing vulnerabilities with the assurance that they will be met with acceptance and validation. Mutual respect becomes the cornerstone, facilitating comfort and security.

One practical approach to fostering this emotional safety involves setting boundaries. Establishing clear boundaries signifies respect for personal space while reinforcing a commitment to understanding one another. It reminds us that it's okay to say "no" or express discomfort and that these expressions safeguard emotional well-being.

Another critical component in nurturing vulnerability involves ritualizing connection. Shared activities and routines create touchpoints for regular emotional sharing, anchoring the relationship in consistency and love. Whether it's a weekly check-in or a creative date night, these rituals provide opportunities to deepen bonds and celebrate the unique individuals within the relationship.

Over time, nurturing vulnerability transforms not only relationships but also individuals. It encourages resilience, builds empathy, and empowers us to face life's complexities. As we embark on this journey, let us remember that vulnerability, far from being a flaw, is a courageous act of strength and an invitation to experience love in its most enriching form. Here's to opening our hearts, embracing the unknown, and discovering the beauty beyond our fears.

Chapter 14

Communicating with Clarity

In the tapestry of human experience, few threads are as deeply interwoven into the fabric of our lives as love and relationships. For young adults standing on the precipice of adulthood, navigating this complex terrain can be as exhilarating as daunting. At an age where emotions run deep, and connections shape our understanding of the world, the quest for authentic love becomes both a challenge and an adventure. Welcome to a journey through the nuances of vulnerability—a path that leads to deeper emotional intimacy and transformative self-discovery.

At its core, vulnerability is more than just letting someone in; it's about showing up as our most authentic selves and daring to share our dreams, fears, and desires. It invites us to drop the masks and armor we've constructed over time and embrace the raw, unfiltered essence of who we are. This openness, though scary at times, has the potential to forge connections so profound that they redefine what it means to know and be known by another person.

Yet despite its undeniable power, vulnerability often gets a bad rap. Many of us grow up equating it with weakness, taught to guard our hearts and shield ourselves from emotional exposure. But what if, instead, we saw vulnerability as strength? What if being honest about our feelings wasn't something to be feared but celebrated? By embracing this mindset, we open the door to relationships built on trust and mutual respect, where authenticity reigns supreme.

Throughout history, countless love stories have demonstrated the unparalleled strength that arises from vulnerability. Take the couple who, amidst the chaos of life, decided to share their insecurities and found solace in doing so. Their shared vulnerability became the balm that soothed their fears, allowing them to face challenges together and emerge stronger. Or consider the pair who learned that expressing their needs and concerns honestly prevented misunderstandings and cultivated a culture of open dialogue. These narratives illuminate the transformative power of vulnerability, serving as beacons of hope and inspiration.

But embracing vulnerability isn't always easy. The fear of emotional exposure is a formidable barrier that many grapple with. The voice whispers caution, urging us to stay concealed and safe. Yet, ironically, it's through confronting these fears that we find liberation. By recognizing the patterns of avoidance that hold us back and reframing vulnerability as an opportunity for growth, we dismantle the walls that hinder fair connection.

Contrary to popular belief, emotional exposure is not a reckless leap into the unknown. Instead, it's a calculated step towards authenticity—exploring oneself and one's relationship with others. By perceiving vulnerability as a pathway to meaningful connections, we cultivate a mindset that celebrates emotional risks. We learn that each act of openness, no matter how small, marks progress toward decent relationships. Sharing personal anecdotes and celebrating these moments of courage encourages us to venture further down this path.

Integral to embracing vulnerability is establishing honest communication, the foundation of trust. In relationships, honesty isn't merely about truthfulness—it's about creating an environment where both partners feel secure in voicing thoughts and emotions without fearing judgment. Active listening plays a pivotal role here, fostering a sense of being heard and valued. When we fully engage with our partner's words, we create a space where deeper emotions can surface and be understood.

Furthermore, expressing our needs openly is vital. Addressing concerns early prevents simmering issues from boiling over later, ensuring trust remains intact. When integrated into every facet of a relationship, communication acts like regular maintenance, keeping the lines of connection solid and resilient.

Creating a safe space where vulnerability can thrive requires intention and effort. It's about building an emotional sanctuary where judgments are left at the door, and empathy takes center stage. Such environments allow partners to be themselves, sharing vulnerabilities with the assurance that they will be met with acceptance and validation. Mutual respect becomes the cornerstone, facilitating comfort and security.

One practical approach to fostering this emotional safety involves setting boundaries. Establishing clear boundaries signifies respect for personal space while reinforcing a commitment to understanding one another. It reminds us that it's okay to say "no" or express discomfort and that these expressions safeguard emotional well-being.

Another critical component in nurturing vulnerability involves ritualizing connection. Shared activities and routines create touchpoints for regular emotional sharing, anchoring the relationship in consistency and love. Whether it's a weekly check-in or a creative date night, these rituals provide opportunities to deepen bonds and celebrate the unique individuals within the relationship.

Over time, nurturing vulnerability transforms not only relationships but also individuals. It encourages resilience, builds empathy, and empowers us to face life's complexities. As we embark on this journey, let us remember that vulnerability, far from being a flaw, is a courageous act of strength and an invitation to experience love in its most enriching form. Here's to opening our hearts, embracing the unknown, and discovering the beauty beyond our fears.

chapter 15

Fostering Emotional Resilience

In the intricate dance of young adulthood, romance often emerges as a song and a silence—a melody weaving through our sometimes harmonious experiences and other times discordant. Emotional resilience is at the heart of these experiences, a concept frequently referenced yet not always understood in its proper depth. Imagine stepping into the world of love armed with eagerness or hope and a robust emotional toolkit that enables you to handle whatever comes your way. We embark on this journey together, exploring how transformative resilience can be in navigating romantic complexities.

Picture this: You're captivated by someone new, and each exchanged a smile, and the shared moment is electric. But then, inevitably, challenges arise—miscommunication, unmet expectations, heartbreak. It's easy to feel overwhelmed, wanting to retreat into layers of self-preservation. Here's where understanding emotional resilience becomes crucial. Defined, it's the ability to adapt and recover from life's inevitable difficulties. In romantic relationships, the armor protects you from succumbing to despair when faced with conflicts or disappointments. It's not about being unaffected by what happens but rather about rising above and maintaining mental well-being amidst stress.

Consider emotional resilience as a muscle, one that strengthens with intentional use. The more you exercise it, the more equipped you are for love's roller coaster ride. Building this skill directly influences relationship satisfaction and longevity. Instead of perceiving setbacks as failures, resilient individuals view them as opportunities for learning and growth. They navigate love's labyrinthine paths with mindful awareness, cherishing moments of happiness while embracing the bumps along the way as part of the journey.

Take a moment and reflect: What personal strengths have carried you through tricky times? Identifying these resilient qualities within yourself is empowering. Think back to challenges overcome, whether romantic or otherwise, and acknowledge those victories. Each experience contributes to a more resilient mindset, laying a foundation for handling future uncertainties confidently and gracefully. Recognizing your inherent strength fosters greater self-awareness, which is invaluable in maintaining healthy relationships.

It's also vital to recognize how societal norms might shape your perspective on resilience. Cultural expectations often influence how we approach and perceive love, sometimes undermining our emotional strength without realizing it. Awareness of these external factors allows you to consciously cultivate resilience, trusting your agency to shape your romantic experiences. You empower yourself to build balanced, authentic relationships by disentangling personal beliefs from societal pressures.

Experiencing rejection or heartbreak is a universal rite of passage in love. Yet, learning how to cope effectively with such challenges is rarely taught. Rejection doesn't define your worth; instead, it offers a poignant opportunity for growth. Viewing these painful experiences not as failures but as essential steps in personal development reframes your narrative positively. It opens the door to learning, understanding, and strengthening emotional resilience.

Processing emotions, especially heartbreak, requires a healthy outlet. Whether through writing, art, or conversations with trusted friends, openly expressing feelings aids in healing. It's crucial to validate emotions—letting them surface without shame or judgment prevents them from decaying unproductively. Constructive emotional expression releases pent-up frustration, allowing you to move forward with renewed clarity and purpose.

In keeping perspective, remember that love is a journey, not a destination. Each romantic encounter, regardless of outcome, enriches your life's tapestry. Not every connection will lead to forever, but every story adds value, teaching you something new about yourself and what you desire in future relationships. Focusing on the future instead of dwelling solely on past regrets fosters hope, encouraging a resilient outlook where optimism thrives.

Building a solid support network during trying times further enhances resilience. Friends and family offer diverse perspectives and much-needed comfort during heartbreak. Sharing vulnerability strengthens community bonds, reinforcing that you are never alone in your experiences. Whether leaning on a best friend or seeking guidance from mentors, surrounding yourself with love and understanding bolsters your emotional fortitude.

As you navigate the aftermath of setbacks, prioritizing self-care is paramount. Engaging in activities that bring joy and fulfillment rejuvenates the spirit. Embrace hobbies, indulge in creative passions, or immerse yourself in physical pursuits like exercise—all of which contribute significantly to emotional recovery. These acts of self-nurturing remind you of your worth independent of relationship status.

Mindfulness practices, too, play a pivotal role in emotional recovery. By fostering an attitude of reflection, you gain insight into past actions and decisions, transforming regret into valuable lessons. Consider gratitude exercises to shift focus from loss to appreciation for growth and wisdom accrued. Such practices ground you in the present, allowing you to emerge stronger, wiser, and ready to embrace future possibilities with open arms.

At times, professional help may provide additional support. Therapy or counseling offers a safe space to explore deeper emotional processing, equipping you with strategies tailored to your unique circumstances. Normalizing the pursuit of mental health reinforces proactive efforts toward healing, underscoring the courage it takes to seek assistance when needed.

Remember, setbacks in love offer profound opportunities for learning and self-discovery. Adopting a growth mindset empowers you to transform pain into purpose, whether through activism, storytelling, or creative endeavors. As you share your narrative, you contribute to a collective understanding that strengthens community ties and inspires resilience in others facing similar challenges.

Ultimately, the experiences you encounter shape the resilient identity you carry forward. Embrace the adaptability gained through weathering life's storms, affirming your strength and tenacity in each step. Through resilience, you enhance your capacity to love and be entwined together and cultivate a sense of enduring hope—knowing that every chapter unfolds with promise and potential, fueled by the beautiful complexity of love itself

Chapter 16

Building Mutual Respect

In a world where every heartbeat feels like a countdown to something extraordinary, young love unfolds with the drama and intensity of a movie scene. Imagine the mystery of midnight conversations punctuated by laughter, the exhilaration of holding hands under the stars, or the moment your heart races because you're finally close enough to them that the rest of the world fades away. Love at this age is raw, powerful, and transformative. Yet, as intoxicating as it can be, navigating the waters of romance without a map can also lead to stormy seas.

Welcome to understanding what makes relationships survive and thrive amid life's complexities. At the heart of every successful partnership lies a fundamental element—mutual respect. It's more than just a word or a checkbox on a list of relationship goals; it's the bedrock upon which trust, communication, and equality stand tall. For those moments when you're wondering whether your love story will sweep you off your feet or leave you on shaky ground, mutual respect could be your guiding light.

So, what exactly does respect look like between two people in love? It might resemble a familiar scene: valuing each other's feelings when emotions run high, appreciating differing opinions even during disagreements, or understanding boundaries that protect both partners' well-being. Respect transforms a relationship from a mere interaction into a profound connection. It means genuinely listening to your partner's dreams, fears, and opinions and creating a safe space for them to express themselves authentically.

But respect doesn't just happen; it requires conscious effort and often means setting aside personal egos. It's essential to differentiate respect from control. In a loving relationship, one person doesn't rule over the other; instead, they walk side by side, supporting each other's aspirations. This kind of partnership isn't about dictating choices but encouraging autonomy, knowing that true love roots for each person's growth as an individual.

Imagine a couple earnestly celebrating each other's triumphs, big or small. Whether it's acing an exam, landing a dream job, or simply making it through a tough day, these moments matter. Genuine admiration and support are everyday acts that speak volumes about respect. When respect thrives, misunderstandings and conflicts find little room to grow, and starkly contrasting relationships where respect is absent lead to bitterness, resentment, and power imbalances.

Setting boundaries is an equally critical aspect of any relationship. Think of boundaries as an invisible line drawn not to separate but to protect each partner's emotional and psychological space. They serve as personal guidelines, ensuring both partners feel respected and secure. For instance, expressing your boundaries using "I" statements can prevent misunderstandings and create an environment where both partners feel heard and valued. Revisit these boundaries as the relationship evolves, allowing them to adapt naturally to new stages and experiences.

Respect extends far beyond recognizing boundaries; it includes honoring them. Ignoring or violating these boundaries can sow seeds of discord and erode trust. However, once a foundation of respect is laid, discussing boundaries becomes a pathway for growth and intimacy.

As we delve deeper, we encounter another unavoidable facet of relationships: disagreements. Yes, they happen, even in the most respectful partnerships. The real test is how we handle these conflicts. Do they turn into battlegrounds or stepping stones for greater understanding? Engaging respectfully means using conflicts as opportunities for growth, always focusing on the issue rather than resorting to personal attacks.

Active listening becomes your secret weapon here. Reflecting on what's been said, avoiding interruptions, and striving to understand before reacting—these practices transform conflicts into dialogues. Sometimes, humor diffuses tension, making you realize that maybe it wasn't such a big deal after all. Post-disagreement, reflecting on what worked and what didn't, ensures that future conflicts yield more productive outcomes.

Finally, imagine a partnership built on equality—a delicate yet empowering balance that propels both individuals forward. Equality doesn't mean splitting everything precisely down the middle. Instead, it recognizes each partner's unique strengths and contributions, fostering a dynamic where both feel valued and capable. Sharing responsibilities equitably avoids the pitfalls of resentment and cultivates teamwork. It's about supporting each other's dreams and aspirations, encouraging personal growth, and nurturing collective goals that strengthen the vision of a shared future.

When both voices harmonize, expressing ideas and concerns alike, it fosters an environment ripe with collaboration and respect. Here lies the beauty of mutual respect: it paves the way for resilient, loving relationships that defy time and circumstance. As you embark on your love journey, remember that you are always heading toward the shores of understanding, equality, and unwavering partnership with respect as your compass.

This book invites you to explore these themes, offering insights and narratives that echo your experiences and aspirations. Let's navigate together, learning how respect can redefine love, transforming it into a force that empowers and endures.

Chapter 17
Growing Together in Love

Relationships can feel like the wildest roller coaster ride, full of exhilarating highs and nerve-wracking turns. The stakes for young adults navigating this romance thrill ride feel higher than ever. Between the butterflies and the heartbreaks, love in your late teens to early twenties is about growing together, growing individually, and figuring out how to make it work without losing yourself. Welcome to a chapter dedicated to understanding just that: how love and personal evolution go hand in hand in crafting a fulfilling romantic journey.

Imagine you're standing at the edge of a wide-open field, dreams hovering like balloons waiting to be released into the sky. Great partnerships aren't just about holding on to someone's hand; they're about launching those dreams together. It's not enough to dream alone anymore—the real magic happens when mutual encouragement propels you toward ambitions that might have seemed impossible solo. Whether it's an aspiration, you whispered one quiet night, or a grand goal written in journal ink, having someone in your corner who believes in you makes a world of difference. There's something profoundly empowering about the synergy created when partners uplift each other's goals. It's a shared energy that transforms the ordinary into extraordinary.

Picture this: two people rolling up their sleeves, diving into a shared project, whether building a garden in the backyard, starting a small business from scratch, or simply planning an unforgettable road trip. These joint goals are more than activities—they're opportunities to weave your lives together meaningfully. Every step towards achieving these goals deepens that emotional connection, turning partners into allies. The essence of being a couple doesn't lie in achieving spectacular feats every day but in celebrating the little triumphs that bind your stories with threads of teamwork and cooperation.

But let's be honest. Life isn't always sunshine and success. Sometimes, things don't go as planned. That's where resilience enters the stage, offering invaluable lessons on navigating setbacks. When life throws curveballs—and it will—how you handle them together defines the strength of your bond. A significant aspect of maintaining positivity through disappointments involves keeping communication sincere and open. It's about being there for each other, offering a shoulder to lean on when dreams falter, and finding strength in overcoming challenges. This ability to rise above setbacks can fortify relationships surprisingly, often delivering clarity and unity that only adversity can bring.

Equally important is celebrating individual accomplishments, those personal milestones that demand applause and recognition. Celebrating these moments engenders a culture of appreciation and pride within the relationship. When you recognize your partner's achievements, whether big or small, you affirm their worth and contribution, creating an environment where both parties can thrive. This acknowledgment enhances morale, ensuring that neither person feels overshadowed or lost in the glow of joint accomplishments.

As time rolls on, change becomes an inevitable companion in any relationship. Adapting to these changes is crucial for survival and blossoming into a partnership that embraces both evolution and intimacy. Relationships naturally transform as individuals grow. Recognizing these subtle shifts requires self-awareness, mature communication, and discussing evolving feelings without fear of conflict. This dialogue nurtures mutual understanding, presenting changes as opportunities rather than obstacles.

Facing transitions gracefully opens doors to new forms of closeness. Embracing changes can foster innovation in how partners relate, creating space for innovative forms of intimacy. Even amid shifting landscapes, emotional bonds can remain intact, fortified by shared experiences during moments of transition. Quality time becomes even more valuable, an anchor of stability during changing tides, emphasizing connection despite external transformations.

Of course, what's a relationship without joy? Celebrating victories together enhances the spirit of positivity and appreciation. Think about the traditions and celebratory rituals you can create, amplifying happiness and weaving joy throughout your narrative. Whether a small accomplishment or a significant milestone, these celebrations solidify emotional connections, making lasting memories.

Listening actively, sharing history, and understanding diverse perspectives allow partners to deepen their connection. Each conversation about past experiences can enrich understanding, foster empathy, and resolve conflicts. Sharing vulnerabilities isn't easy, but it creates a safe foundation upon which deeper intimacy can grow. Incorporating diverse perspectives enables couples to make informed decisions, leveraging unique backgrounds to enrich discussions and problem-solving.

Ultimately, the key lies in synthesizing these shared learnings into actionable insights that enhance the relationship. Growth becomes continuous, guided by the knowledge gained from mutual experiences. Adjusting behaviors based on these insights nurtures stronger ties, setting the stage for future adventures together.

By the end of this book, we aim for you to walk away with the tools and insights needed to nurture a partnership that is surviving and thriving—one that grows stronger with each challenge and blooms brighter with every shared success. As you flip through these chapters, may you find the inspiration to support one another's dreams, adapt to life's inevitable changes, celebrate each victory, and treasure the beautiful complexities of love's journey.

chapter 18

Balancing Independence and Togetherness

Finding equilibrium can feel like balancing on a tightrope in a world where young hearts constantly learn the intricate dance of love and independence. Love is exhilarating and consuming, yet it requires more than passion to thrive. It demands understanding and a delicate balance between togetherness and individuality. For those of us navigating these tumultuous waters, mastering this balance becomes crucial—not just for our romantic relationships but also for our personal growth.

Imagine stepping into a relationship with two powerful forces: the desire to be one with your partner and the innate need to remain true to yourself. It's a universal dilemma, transcending age and experience, but particularly poignant among young adults. At a stage in life where identity is still being sculpted, allowing space for personal expression and nurturing a relationship can often seem contradictory. But embracing this contradiction forms the very essence of a healthy bond.

Picture your favorite musician spinning a melody, harmonizing distinct notes into a beautiful symphony. Relationships should work similarly. Each person brings their rhythm and instruments, creating a melody when they play together. However, maintaining harmony requires patience, empathy, and clarity. As you find yourself lost in the embrace of love, it's essential not to lose sight of your song—your identity.

Why does personal space matter so much? Let's dive deeper. The idea of personal space often conjures images of physical distance, but it's about setting emotional boundaries, too. It's a sanctuary where each partner can recharge—the quiet moments spent delving into hobbies, reflecting on thoughts, or simply lounging in solitude. In these moments of withdrawal, we rediscover our passions, realign our goals, and emerge ready to pour renewed energy into the partnership.

When you respect your partner's need for solitude, you're not fostering separation but sowing the seeds for a stronger connection. Appreciating alone time doesn't mean disregarding your partner—it's about acknowledging that this space breathes life into love, preventing it from becoming suffocating. With individual experiences, each partner adds richness to shared moments, making conversations vibrant and bonds unbreakable.

Setting boundaries around this space plays a crucial role. Communicating openly about what you need creates an environment where both partners feel valued and respected. Discussing expectations helps mitigate misunderstandings and prevents feelings of neglect. It might feel uncomfortable initially, but addressing and respecting these boundaries cultivates a sense of safety and trust, empowering both individuals to be genuine selves within the relationship.

Transitioning between shared experiences and solitary pursuits can sometimes feel like juggling fire. Yet mastering this transition can bring about immense personal and relational growth. Imagine having deep discussions about how much time you each need for yourselves versus time spent together. These conversations allow both partners to feel heard and understood, further fueling the intimacy that binds them.

Let's explore the importance of balancing solo life and relationship commitments. Establishing routines can be your guiding star here. Creating a schedule that allocates time for joint activities and personal endeavors strengthens the connection without compromising individuality. Planned personal time provides stability, ensuring neither aspect of life is overshadowed by the other. Routines remind us that while love is spontaneous, maintaining it sometimes requires conscientious planning.

Much like any masterpiece, a relationship thrives on variety. While some may crave a night out dancing together, others might prefer losing themselves in a book alone. Respecting these differing interests means recognizing that pursuing separate passions doesn't signify division; instead, it broadens horizons and enriches interactions with newfound stories to share.

This way, effective time management becomes your ally. Planners or apps can help ensure that chores get done and that there's room for self-care alongside bonding activities. By prioritizing essential relationship events and offering flexibility in scheduling, you create an atmosphere where both partners can pursue their interests without guilt or resentment.

As you tread this path together, continuous dialogue ensures no unmet need festers into frustration. Regular check-ins encourage sharing feelings regarding time balance, allowing adjustments that align with evolving needs. This openness fosters understanding and strengthens the intricate fabric of your relationship.

Encouraging each other's independence isn't just beneficial—it's integral. Celebrating your partner's achievements and milestones boosts confidence and validation, building a nurturing environment where both can flourish. Recognizing and supporting personal time demonstrates respect, promoting a profound appreciation for each other's ambitions.

Avoiding co-dependency is vital to sustaining a healthy relationship. When both partners embrace their independence, they cultivate healthier emotional states, enhancing the connection without diminishing their identities. Understanding and accepting personal limitations aid growth, free from resentment's shadow.

In fostering an atmosphere conducive to autonomy, establishing trust becomes paramount. Open discussions about potential insecurities or jealousy can demystify these emotions, paving the way for reassurance during personal pursuits. Strength lies in knowing that despite time apart, the foundation remains steadfast.

Finally, let's recognize the beauty in differences. Embracing unique perspectives informs richer conversations and enhances problem-solving capabilities, strengthening the relationship's core. When approached constructively, differences become catalysts for growth and innovation, infusing new life into even familiar dynamics.

Compromise plays an equally pivotal role in maintaining harmony. Learning when to yield reinforces mutual respect and teamwork, fortifying the partnership against external challenges. In successfully resolving conflicts, partners reinforce resilience, preparing them for future obstacles.

Creating space for open dialogue ensures individual voices aren't lost. Regular conversations about differing views foster understanding before judgment arises, removing barriers and celebrating diversity within unity.

Ultimately, embracing these principles leads to a fulfilling partnership. A relationship where personal space is honored nurtures individuality and connection, laying the groundwork for a thriving, loving journey that transforms lives and hearts.

chapter 19

Finding Strength in Adversity

Navigating the world of young love can often feel like a breathtaking rollercoaster—packed with thrilling highs, stomach-churning lows, and unexpected twists. For many young adults, these early relationship experiences are both exhilarating and daunting, filled with moments that shape our perceptions of love and resilience. This book guides that journey, capturing the essence of young romance woven together with personal growth.

What if we could transform the inevitable challenges and conflicts in relationships into stepping stones toward stronger, deeper connections? Picture this: two individuals standing against life's trials, united by affection and shared strength and understanding. The tumultuous periods of any relationship don't have to drive us apart. Instead, they can become the glue that binds us closer, forging bonds that withstand the test of time.

Whether you're facing the strains of long distances during college or grappling with misunderstandings that threaten harmony, learning to approach adversity as a team could redefine your relationship's trajectory. Imagine brainstorming with your partner—not just about daily plans but strategies to overcome these hurdles together. When you're side by side in tackling life's obstacles, you discover an emotional connection more profound than before. Collaboration breeds unity and a sense of belonging, turning adversities into mutual victories rather than bitter defeats.

And let's not forget the crucial role communication plays. In those moments when it feels like you're speaking different languages, open dialogue becomes your lifeline. It's not just about talking but sharing with honesty and vulnerability, allowing both fears and dreams to surface. Through this sincere exchange, you create a sanctuary where both partners feel seen and respected. Miscommunications that once seemed daunting morph into opportunities for clarity and connection, deepening your cultivated trust.

Considering varying perspectives also holds significant power during testing times. Differences in opinion might initially seem like chasms to bridge, yet they can be incredibly enriching. By welcoming diverse viewpoints, you're nurturing respect and fostering a partnership built on creativity and adaptability. These variances in thought propel you towards novel solutions and innovative ways of connecting, further solidifying your bond.

In the whirlwind of growing together, celebrating even the most minor victories can inject positivity into the relationship dynamic. Every little milestone achieved is worth acknowledging because it reinforces the spirit of encouragement and motivation. Whether getting through a tough week or resolving a minor disagreement, each triumph fuels the overarching narrative of love flourishing amid adversity.

Moreover, conflicts don't have to spell disaster; they can catalyze emotional and relational growth. Shifting your mindset to view disagreements as opportunities rather than barriers paves the way for constructive conversations that spark change. Delving into what lies beneath these disputes helps unravel personal triggers and reactions, presenting a chance for self-improvement and growth.

Setting shared goals based on past conflicts prevents recurring issues and provides a clear direction for future interactions. Together, you carve a path forward, where mutual aspirations guide the following steps, ensuring transparency and alignment. Empathy becomes your compass in this journey, guiding you to listen beyond words and truly grasp your partner's perspective. This culture of empathy fosters love and support even amidst differences, nurturing an environment where disputes become bridges to understanding rather than divisive walls.

Rebuilding trust after hitting rough patches demands dedication and patience—a gentle reminder that healing is a process, not an immediate fix. Acknowledging mistakes with sincerity takes courage, but it lays the groundwork for mending any rift. Consistency in actions reinforces reliability and commitment, slowly restoring faith in the relationship's foundation.

Creating an environment conducive to forgiveness is essential in moving forward positively. By establishing mechanisms for open dialogue, couples can navigate the complexities of apologies and healing without falling into repetitive conflict cycles. Over time, patient efforts cultivate renewed trust, underscoring the belief that any relationship can rise from its ashes more robust than before.

In the healing phase, mutual support and understanding form the bedrock upon which renewed connections thrive. Being present for each other in need strengthens ties and dispels isolation. Creating shared empathetic moments enriches emotional intimacy, allowing partners to delve into each other's emotional landscapes with compassion and care.

Seeking professional guidance can provide fresh insights and equip couples with practical tools for navigating their journey. External perspectives offer support in such spaces, normalizing the shared human experience of relationship struggles. Establishing a haven for vulnerability ensures both partners can freely express fears and emotions, reinforcing the trust-filled environment vital for long-lasting connection.

As you journey through the chapters of this book, you'll uncover ways to embrace love's challenges as powerful avenues for growth and transformation. We invite you to explore these narratives of resilience and hope—stories that echo the collective experiences of young adults stepping into the world of love armed with newfound strength and understanding.

chapter 20

Realizing the Transformative Power of Love

In a world where young minds' heartbeats synchronize with love's rhythms, we find stories that resonate with our deepest desires for connection. As young adults navigating the often tumultuous waters of romance and relationships, you embark on a journey where love is both the compass and the destination. In these early years, one experiences the intoxicating highs and heart-wrenching lows of love, all while seeking the wisdom to steer through its complexities.

This book invites you to explore the transformative power of love—a profound force that reshapes who you are and how you view the world. Love is not merely an emotion but a catalyst for change and growth. It whispers to you in moments of solitude, encouraging a shift in your mindset and prompting you to see life through hope and positivity. When love enters your life, it can color even the darkest days with shades of optimism, offering you a hand to hold during life's most challenging times. Imagine a relationship where encouragement is woven into every conversation, creating an unyielding foundation of support.

As you engage with the narratives within these pages, you'll discover that love opens doors to emotional growth and maturity. In the simple act of being in love, you learn to identify and embrace your emotions, fostering a deeper understanding of yourself and those around you. This journey of self-discovery is aided by the empathy and patience cultivated through shared experiences—the laughter, the tears, the quiet moments of reflection. Such emotional intelligence equips you to navigate life's intricate web of relationships with grace and resilience.

Moreover, love is an incredible way of enhancing your self-image in a world that often challenges your sense of worth, and having someone who believes in your potential can be transformative. The gentle affirmations from a partner can bolster your confidence and empower you to pursue dreams you once deemed unattainable. You'll find comfort in knowing that you deserve happiness and affection, a realization that fuels your achievements and encourages you to confront insecurities with bravery.

With love as your motivator, you may feel a renewed drive to chase after your goals. Whether pursuing higher education, exploring career opportunities, or simply becoming the best version of yourself, love inspires growth. It celebrates each milestone with you, making success all the more fulfilling when shared. Together, partners set aspirations and work tirelessly towards them, strengthening their bond and nurturing a partnership built on progress and mutual support.

This exploration also delves into the indelible link between love and resilience. Life is rife with obstacles, but with love by your side, challenges become growth opportunities. A loving relationship provides a sanctuary, a haven where you feel secure enough to face adversity head-on. This emotional safety net allows you to explore your vulnerabilities without fear, knowing that your partner stands beside you, ready to weather any storm together. Love's ability to foster resilience extends beyond individual strength; it binds you together in times of need, empowering you to rely on shared strengths to overcome life's hurdles.

Couples often develop collective coping mechanisms, learning to address stress and setbacks as a team. The journey of overcoming difficulties deepens trust and commitment, leaving both partners better equipped to navigate future trials. With every triumph over adversity, love instills a belief that challenges, rather than breaking us, can lead to personal and relational growth.

Ultimately, loving relationships bring a sense of fulfillment that transcends ordinary experiences. There's a unique joy in knowing that love contributes to your purpose, granting your life a direction rooted in togetherness. With love, you create memories etched in time, moments that paint a portrait of a life well-lived. These connections ripple outward, touching communities and extending networks of support.

Within these pages, you'll find tales of resilience and growth, of love that builds bridges and ignites a passion for life. The legacy of love created by these stories transcends generations, setting examples for nurturing future relationships and strengthening societal bonds.

So, take this journey with open hearts and curious minds. Let the stories unfold, showing you that love is a fleeting sentiment and a powerful force that can elevate your life, fill you with purpose, and weave a tapestry of fulfillment. Welcome to a world where love is the ultimate storyteller—let it inspire and guide you toward a future full of possibility and promise.

Conclusion

As you open the pages of this book, take a moment to imagine yourself on a journey. It's a journey through love and relationships, an adventure that mirrors the experiences of many young adults today. This book is your guide, helping you navigate the sometimes stormy seas of romance with relatable narratives reflecting your experiences. Whether you're tangled up in first loves, navigating heartbreaks, or simply trying to understand the complexities of emotions that come with being in a relationship, we've got you covered.

In these chapters, you'll find stories and insights specially crafted for young adults like you, aged 16-24. You're at a stage in life where relationships can be both exhilarating and challenging. You're exploring what it means to connect deeply with someone else while figuring out who you are. Through engaging narratives, we'll walk with you, offering guidance on managing the emotional depths of love and the intricacies of relationships.

Perhaps you've already tasted the sweetness of love or felt its sting. Maybe you're drawn to stories where personal growth and romance intertwine, highlighting resilience and love's transformative power. This book speaks to that, acknowledging the hurdles of young love and celebrating the growth that emerges from overcoming them. It serves as a mirror reflecting your experiences and a map lighting the path forward.

Think of each chapter as a conversation—a heart-to-heart chat about themes and lessons that resonate deeply with our shared human experience. We'll delve into the importance of communication, opening those lines to foster deeper connections. You'll read about vulnerability and how embracing it paves the way for genuine bonds. Remember, feeling exposed is okay; it's a sign of courage, not weakness.

From the very first chapter, we explore personal insecurities and how they impact relationships. Building self-confidence is paramount; it forms the backbone of letting your guard down around others. When you believe in yourself, you become more willing to share your true self, flaws and all, with someone special. This willingness to open up invites emotional intimacy—something far more prosperous and enduring than mere infatuation.

But let's be honest: Love isn't always rainbows and butterflies. Relationships are filled with challenges that test patience, trust, and understanding. The beauty lies in the resilience you cultivate when facing these obstacles. As we peel back the layers of romantic entanglements, we highlight the joy and struggles. We honor your resolve to navigate your path and learn from each experience, no matter how difficult it may seem.

Through tales of love, found and lost, these chapters offer lessons to tuck into the corners of your heart. How do conflicts shape us? What does it mean to compromise, indeed? In answering these questions, you'll see examples of love as a catalyst for change, urging partners to grow alongside each other. These narratives aim to inspire you, encouraging introspection and, ultimately, transformation.

Now, you might wonder how to apply this to your life. That's where the magic happens. Throughout these pages, you'll gather wisdom to empower you, enabling you to approach your relationships with a renewed perspective. It is a toolkit for facing romantic challenges, armed with understanding, empathy, and courage.

Your task is to absorb these insights and weave them into your story. Approach your relationships intentionally, with maturity and bravery. Be present for every high, every low, and every lesson learned along the way. Understand that in each interaction, there's potential for growth—for you and for the bond you share with others.

This book doesn't claim to have all the answers because, truthfully, love remains one of life's greatest mysteries. However, as you digest these pages, we hope to provide clarity and comfort, much like a friend lending an ear or offering advice. Together, we'll explore what it means to love deeply, authentically, and fearlessly.

When you close this book, may you feel inspired and encouraged? Hold tightly to the knowledge and insights gained here, ready to face whatever comes next in your romantic endeavors with a fuller understanding of yourself and what it means to connect with others truly.

So, as you embark on this literary voyage, allow yourself to be vulnerable. Let these words wash over you, sparking reflections on past relationships and dreams of those yet to come. Embrace the possibility of change and growth at every turn. This is your journey, and every step you take leads to more profound love and understanding—not just of others but of yourself.

Let's dive into this journey together, exploring the transformative power of love and your strength to overcome any obstacle. Welcome to a narrative woven with emotion, resilience, and growth—a story that celebrates love in all its wondrous, sometimes perplexing beauty.

ABOUT THE AUTHOR

Willy Lapse Laguerre is a passionate storyteller whose work explores the depths of human connection and the complexities of love. With a keen eye for detail and a heart attuned to the intricacies of emotion, Willy's writing captures the beauty and challenges of relationships that transcend boundaries.

Drawing inspiration from his experiences and the world, Willy creates profoundly personal and universally resonant narratives. His stories invite readers to journey into realms where love defies convention and characters grapple with profound questions of identity, belonging, and purpose.

When he's not writing, Willy enjoys immersing himself in literature, exploring new cultures, and seeking moments of quiet reflection that fuel his creative process. *Unveiling a Love That Defies Conventions* is a testament to his dedication to storytelling and belief in love's transformative power.

Willy currently resides in Berlin, Germany, where he continues to craft tales that inspire and captivate readers worldwide.

Don't miss out!

Visit the website below and you can sign up to receive emails whenever Willy Lapse Laguerre publishes a new book. There's no charge and no obligation.

https://books2read.com/r/B-A-QNFNC-OZYHF

BOOKS 2 READ

Connecting independent readers to independent writers.

Did you love *Healing Hearts In The Shadows Of Forbidden Love*? Then you should read *The Game You Can Never Win*[1] by Willy Lapse Laguerre!

[2]

Summary and Reflections

This journey explored the essential elements needed to form deep and meaningful connections. We discussed how setting clear intentions can lay a strong foundation for trust and authenticity in relationships. By practicing active engagement, like listening carefully and showing genuine interest, we can make others feel valued and respected. Embracing vulnerability is also crucial; opening up and sharing personal experiences allows for a more profound understanding and empathy between individuals. Revisiting meaningful conversations ensures relationships remain dynamic and adaptable to change,

1. https://books2read.com/u/bOqNpK

2. https://books2read.com/u/bOqNpK

providing opportunities to address unresolved issues and celebrate progress. Looking ahead, it's clear that relationships thrive on consistency and openness. Regular communication acts as the lifeline connecting partners, fostering a sense of trust and mutual respect. Being transparent and accountable reinforces our commitment to the relationship, making each partner feel secure. Celebrating shared milestones and embracing diverse perspectives further enriches the connection, adding layers of depth and understanding. Cultivating satisfying connections requires patience and dedication, like tending to a growing plant. Investing time and effort while respecting individuality creates an environment where relationships can flourish authentically and robustly.

to reconsider their approaches to competition, ambition, and life's uncertain journey.

www.ingramcontent.com/pod-product-compliance
Lightning Source LLC
LaVergne TN
LVHW091103150826
845673LV00002B/708